BEING A PERSON

Being a Person

Where Faith and Science Meet

John Habgood

Hodder & Stoughton

LONDON SYDNEY AUCKLAND

Scripture quotations are taken from the Holy Bible,
Authorised King James Version, copyright of the Crown;
and the Revised English Bible, copyright © 1989 by
Oxford University Press and Cambridge University Press

First published in Great Britain in 1998

10 9 8 7 6 5 4 3 2 1

British Library Cataloguing in Publication Data
A record for this book is available from the British Library

ISBN 0 340 69073 9

Typeset by Avon Dataset Ltd, Bidford-on-Avon, Warks

Printed and bound in Great Britain by
Mackays of Chatham, Chatham, Kent

Hodder and Stoughton Ltd
A Division of Hodder Headline PLC
338 Euston Road
London NW1 3BH

In gratitude to family and friends
for the experience of learning together
what it means to be a person

Contents

Acknowledgments

While every effort has been made to contact the copyright holders of material used in this book, this has not always been successful. Full acknowledgment will gladly be made in any future editions.

I am grateful to those concerned for permission to use the following quotations: on p. 8 Copyright © 1960 *The Informed Heart* by Bruno Bettelheim, Thames and Hudson, London; on p. 55 Copyright © 1986 Elizabeth Jennings, *In a Garden*, from *Collected Poems*, Carcanet Press, Manchester; on p. 119 Copyright © 1989 Steven Connor, *Postmodernist Culture*, Blackwell, Oxford; on p. 172 Copyright © Keith Devlin 1997 the words beginning 'Susan saw...' from *Goodbye Descartes*, John Wiley and Sons, New York; on pp. 196–7 Copyright © 1993 from *The Passion of Michel Foucault* by James Miller, Flamingo, reproduced by permission of Greene and Heaton Ltd.

Preface

This book is a much expanded version of the Riddell Lectures, delivered at the University of Newcastle in January 1997. I am grateful to the University for inviting me to participate in this distinguished lecture series on Science and Religion, for its generous hospitality, and for managing to provide such an impressive mixed audience on three successive evenings.

Lectures and books on science and religion tend to concentrate on a number of well-worn themes, some of which will inevitably be found in these pages. In choosing to discuss the nature of persons I was deliberately selecting a topic which is straddled by many disciplines, and in which some dialogue between scientific and religious insights is inevitable, if only because questions about who or what we are cannot be fitted into neat academic categories. There are, of course, many books on the nature of human personality, not surprisingly because the subject is central to human life. Nor is it surprising that there should be many academic disciplines relevant to the study of personhood, because almost every area of human interest impinges on what we are, and how we understand ourselves. The topic is therefore huge.

My excuse for adding to the literature is that, while there is much specialised writing on the subject, I am not aware of any modest, non-technical book for general readers, which draws on a range of different disciplines, and endeavours to make some connections from a Christian point of view. My aim is to reveal something of the many-sidedness of questions about what persons are, and to suggest that theology may have a crucial role in holding these different insights and perspectives together. I have centred my reflections on two urgent, practical questions in the field of medical ethics, one concerning the Persistent Vegetative State, the other to do with abortion: one about the end of human life, the other about the beginning of it. Different aspects of these questions recur at various points throughout the book, and are intended to give it a unity of focus, despite the many themes discussed.

Chapter 1 introduces some of the main issues through an illustration from the world of literature, linking four stages in the modern questioning of personal identity. Writers, even children's writers, often have sensitive antennae which can detect the first tremors of earthquakes to come. Chapter 2 is also introductory, and is a preliminary exploration of the two main problems in medical ethics, which also raise profound questions about personal identity, and around which the book is constructed. Chapters 3, 4 and 5 are mainly historical, giving a brief description of the development of the concept of personhood, and in particular the two poles of individualism and relatedness between which many of the controversies have taken place. Chapter 6 brings the story up to date with a look at present-day bewilderments – notably in postmodernism. The next three chapters, 7, 8 and 9, approach questions about the nature of personhood from a scientific perspective, and review some current ideas about consciousness, the role of language in mental formation, and evolution. Chapter 10 is mainly theological and, together with Chapter 11, argues the main thesis of the book, namely that we cannot fully know what we are as persons without acknowledging the possibilities of self-transcendence – a theme with obvious religious overtones. Chapter 11 sets this discussion in the context of the loss of capacities in old age, and of disasters which damage personality. Chapter 12 looks ahead to ways in which advances in genetics are raising new questions about the nature of personality and the prospects of manipulating the human genetic structure. Chapter 13 points to the inseparability of all these theoretical questions from moral questions about how we relate to our fellow human beings.

There is much more which might have been discussed. I tread lightly through complex philosophical jungles. I say nothing about legal definitions of personhood. My illustrations of the practical implications of different concepts of personhood are drawn from a narrow range – mostly from the field of medical ethics. But I hope that in picking a path through territory familiar to me, I may at least have provided some signposts for others.

I make no special claims to originality, except in the way the material is presented. I have deliberately tried to avoid technical terms, and have often abbreviated arguments to a degree which would not be tolerated in a book with academic pretensions. My main concern has been to provide an accessible introduction to an enormous, and enormously important, subject. For this reason I have excluded footnotes, and provided instead an annotated guide to further reading. This has been deliberately kept short, but it should provide the way in for readers who want to pursue particular themes in more detail.

It remains for me to express respect for the courage and fidelity of Mr and Mrs Bland, whom I have never met, but whose tragic experience set the scene for what I have tried to say. I am also enormously grateful to my friend and former colleague, Raymond Barker, for reading through my penultimate draft and making many helpful suggestions.

Who in the world am I?

As a mathematician, the Reverend Charles Dodgson would have been familiar with some of the strange mathematical speculations which were current in the mid-nineteenth century. The seemingly nonsensical idea of a geometry in which parallel lines can meet would have intrigued him. So would the concept of mathematical logic, which allowed startling conclusions to be derived from innocent-looking premises. I doubt whether it would have occurred to him that this strangeness might be closer to the real world than so-called common sense. He was the sort of man who delighted in mathematical curiosities because they were fun.

He also delighted in children, and because he understood them better than most of his contemporaries, he was able to feel the pressures of the authoritarian and unsympathetic world in which they were usually brought up. He knew about childish fears, and could appreciate how bewildering and threatening so much that went on in the adult world must seem to childish eyes.

Wearing his other hat as Lewis Carroll, he told two stories of sublime nonsense, questioning fundamental assumptions about the secure world, and putting adults, seen in a glorious range of grotesque disguises, in their place. He did it for the entertainment and encouragement of children, but *Alice in Wonderland* and *Alice through the Looking-Glass* have been described by someone, not entirely in jest, as 'the most important philosophical works to come out of Oxford since Duns Scotus (1264–1308)'. While lightheartedly questioning assumptions about ordinary life and logic, the stories also managed to articulate many of the disturbing philosophical issues which were beginning to loom in the nineteenth century and have dominated the twentieth.

Intellectually the nineteenth century was far from complacent. Charles Dodgson took the Dean of Christ Church's daughters for a row on the river and started telling his story only three years after Darwin had published *The Origin of Species*. It was a time when university clerics were under fierce attack. Two years earlier a book of theological essays, *Essays and Reviews*, had drawn public attention in England to the devastating impact of biblical criticism. There were rumblings of social change, and the world of comfortable Oxford dons was being shaken. Yet a basic security remained. Lewis Carroll was able to question the familiar world in play, and to use such questioning in the service of entertainment as if it were a mathematical curiosity. His books are structured as games. Their contents are dreams. We know that Alice will wake up.

Writing some fifty years later, and in the context of

the First World War, Franz Kafka went through a similar process of telling haunting stories in which familiar assumptions were questioned. What would it be like to wake up and find oneself transformed into a gigantic insect, worrying about whether one was going to miss one's morning train? But this was no dream. There was no familiar world to wake up to, just as there were no secure foundations in a European culture in the process of breaking up. Kafka's stories are about the agonising predicament of people in a context where nothing can be taken for granted, and nothing is exactly what it seems. The Czech equivalent of the Victorian child, now an adult, is harried and oppressed by nameless forces in a world no less baffling than the adult world had once seemed to Lewis Carroll's little girls.

Twenty years later Kafka's nightmare became reality in the death camps, the arbitrary trials, the deliberate imposition of meaninglessness on the lives of those selected as the victims of totalitarian regimes. The story of Alice's trial, the sense of bewilderment, the confusion about the past, the mystery about the accusation, the impenetrable proceedings, the awareness that sentence has already been delivered, even before the verdict, might have been told in similar terms in a Kafka novel or a mid-twentieth-century dictator's courtroom.

In our own day the wheel seems to have turned full circle. The questioning of fundamental assumptions has been adopted as a lifestyle in the curious ragbag of late-twentieth-century attitudes lumped together as postmodernism. Some children still live in the twilight world of oppression and abuse, but the majority, at least in Western society, suffer more from lack of guidance than from the all-pervasive moralising against which Lewis Carroll tried to arm them. The key to much present-day bewilderment seems to lie in the assumption that there is no over-arching meaning, but only the ephemeral, the fragmentary, the diverse and the chaotic. It represents a return to playfulness in contrast to purpose. But there is no waking up from this either. Play is the only reality. Life is about 'having fun'.

I first came across this comparison between Lewis Carroll, Kafka and totalitarianism some forty years ago in an article which I have been unable to trace. It has always intrigued me, and seems to contain just enough truth to make it worth exploring a little further. This, at least, is my excuse for turning to Lewis Carroll for some preliminary insights into what it is to be a person in a world where familiar landmarks can no longer be taken for granted.

Alice is in some ways aggressively normal, but she is also anxious and frustrated. Her encounter with the wrong-sized door is an early example of catch-22. Either she is too large to get through it or too small to reach the key on the table. She looks with longing at the garden on the other side, and all her efforts to adapt herself to reach it lead to such alarming changes that she runs into a crisis of identity. The longing for some golden reality beyond reach throws us back on ourselves. 'Who in the world am I?' How do we know that we are ourselves, and not someone else? Perhaps memory is the clue to our identity. But what happens when memory fails? She experiences even deeper alarm in discovering that she can no longer recite multiplication tables or the most familiar poetry. 'How doth the little crocodile . . .' Surely that must be wrong.

This theme of the loss of identity recurs throughout both books. The jurors at Alice's trial write down their names in case they forget them before the end. In the wood of forgetfulness she discovers a new relationship with a fawn as forgetful as herself, a kind of dreaming innocence, which is suddenly shattered by the return of self-consciousness. Tweedledum and Tweedledee taunt her with the thought that she herself is only part of a dream. If the red king was to wake, 'You'd go out – bang! – just like a candle.' There are echoes here of the disturbing thought that our identity exists only in other people's minds. What if they should reject us? Alice meets her rejection when she arrives at her own feast, at a door with 'Queen Alice' written on it, and finds herself locked out, treated as a stranger. 'No admittance till the week after next.'

Alongside these threats to identity is the frustration of a world in which nothing remains as it was. It is impossible to play croquet if the pitch never stays constant and the balls and mallets can walk off when they choose. Without rules there can be no achievements, not even the drastic solutions proposed by that arch-reductionist, the Queen of Hearts: 'Off with his head.' Even words will not stay still, if one is to believe Humpty Dumpty.

Furthermore, the strange characters Alice meets are almost without exception bossy and rude. One might have thought that a caterpillar would have a proper sense of its own lowliness, but not a bit of it. He is the worst of the lot, like an intolerant schoolmaster, with the possible exception of that extreme moraliser, the Duchess. 'Everything's got a moral, if only you can find it.' Alice has to remind herself that in the end they are only a pack of cards.

Beneath all this meaninglessness there is a logic. There are rules to the game. In *Alice through the Looking-Glass* the chess moves are set out at the beginning of the book. Alice herself, despite her worries, manages to remain curious and amused. As in *Cold Comfort Farm*, part of the pleasure of the story lies in the interaction between a fundamentally normal character and the ridiculous turmoil of her surroundings. In Kafka's works, on the other hand, the reader begins to have an uneasy suspicion that the absurd and incomprehensible world being described is all too real. There is only the most tenuous normality with which to contrast it, and even that wears a deceitful face.

Einstein is reputed to have said of Kafka's *The Trial*, 'I couldn't read it; the human mind isn't complicated enough.' The book is nevertheless mesmeric. Every detail is realistic, and the reader is carried along through a world which at first sight seems to be familiar, but is progressively filled with hidden menace. Every scene and character is ambivalent, and the total meaning never becomes clear.

One morning Joseph K. is arrested, and there follows a labyrinthine story of trial and punishment, with no hint of what the crime might be. Is his arrest a joke? a mistake? He attempts reason. He is aware of endless processes going on in the higher reaches of the law, but he does not know the rules, or even if there are any rules.

Near the end, in a scene reminiscent of Alice, he is told a parable by a priest in the cathedral: '. . . before the law stands a doorkeeper. To this doorkeeper there comes a man who begs for admittance to the law. But the doorkeeper says he cannot admit the man at the moment. The man, on reflection, asks if he will be allowed, then, to enter later. "It is possible," answers the doorkeeper, "but not at this moment." Since the door leading to law stands open . . . the man bends down to peer through the entrance . . .' but he is warned off by the doorkeeper with terrifying stories of what lies beyond. So the man settles down to wait . . . and wait . . . until at last, growing old and near death, he asks, ' "Everyone strives to attain the law, how does it come about, then, that in all these years no one has come seeking admittance but me?" "No one but you could gain admittance through this door, since this door was intended only for you. I am now going to shut it." '

There follows a discussion with the priest about what the parable might mean. But this is no help, because no single interpretation does justice to all the details in the story, and the exposition merely becomes more and more convoluted. There are no answers. K. is a man under a curse in a world where there are no secure foundations or interpretations. He is reduced to impotence like a child by forces on which he can get no grip. The reality he faces is all circumference and no centre.

The deliberate imposition of meaninglessness was a

favourite instrument in totalitarian societies for breaking the will to survive. Descriptions of the regime in concentration camps show how the identity of the victims was undermined by treatment which was maliciously unpredictable. Meaningless torture could be followed by meaningless rewards. A status might be given to a prisoner, and then arbitrarily removed. The message constantly hammered home was that these were not real people, whose feelings mattered. They were beings totally at the disposal of their masters, stripped of human dignity by the demonstration that their living and dying was of no consequence.

Bruno Bettelheim, who had first-hand experience of such conditions in the early days of the concentration camps, wrote:

> . . . it was the senseless tasks, the lack of almost any time to oneself, the inability to plan ahead because of sudden changes in camp policies, that was so deeply destructive. By destroying man's ability to act on his own or to predict the outcome of his actions, they destroyed the feeling that his actions had any purpose, so many prisoners stopped acting. But when they stopped acting they soon stopped living. (*The Informed Heart*, p. 148)

Similar experiences were reported by the Lebanese hostages. It was the meaninglessness of their imprisonment, the uncertainty about when (if ever) it would end, and the unpredictability of the treatment they received, which put most strain on their capacities for mental resistance. Brian Keenan describes how his worst periods in captivity were caused by unprovoked violence, not because of the pain but because of the implied disregard of him as a person.

All this is a far cry from Alice. It may seem remote, too, from the conditions of life, at least in Western Europe, on the eve of the millennium. It is nevertheless worth recalling that what we say to ourselves in fun may point to deeper and more sinister realities which have not yet been seen in their full stature. The kind of language commonly used by young people in describing their emotions can serve as an example. The group of youths whose actions resulted in the murder of the headteacher, Philip Lawrence, described how they went out to beat up a victim with the words 'it would be a laugh'. All sorts of people nowadays refer to their unusual, disorderly or daring behaviour as being 'for kicks'. In smart circles it seems that the right way to experience a strong feeling is as 'a surge of adrenalin'. In less smart circles, such as on the programme *Blind Date*, participants rarely say 'I want' or 'I choose', but almost invariably 'It has to be . . .'

This is depersonalising language. Much of it may seem trivial. Some of it may be usefully descriptive. But the overall effect is to disengage feelings and actions from the self, as a person among persons, in favour of a half-mocking quasi-objective stance. Awareness of the self teeters on the edge of meaninglessness, feelings no longer properly 'belong', but at the same time there is a grabbing after raw experience as the only reality. I have already mentioned postmodernism as a sophisticated form of destructive play, and I shall return to this theme later in the book. In the meantime the words of a reviewer in the *Times Literary Supplement*, 12 July 1996, can serve to place it in the context of this chapter. He described himself as scandalised by 'thinkers who consider it their job to track down and eradicate those last vestiges of meaning which address the human world, to dissolve any supposed intrinsic significance of lived experience into an effect of impersonal structures and forces'. He went on to say that there is something distastefully simplistic about postmodernism's 'lazy dismissal of all that went before it as "Western metaphysics" '.

This is what can happen if the subtle indicators which sustain the world of personal meaning are allowed to disappear, whether through playfulness, genuine bewilderment, or deliberate manipulation. Alice could survive in a world of intellectual playfulness because there were still securities which rendered her adventures non-threatening. Kafka barely survived, and the terrible concluding words of *The Trial*, where K. dies – 'Like a dog!' – hammer home the threats to his own personality. Most of the victims of totalitarianism did not survive. What postmodernism will eventually do to us remains to be seen.

I have chosen these four moments of history, as it were, to act as markers in describing a process which extends far beyond them. My concern in this book is how we understand ourselves as persons, and the moral implications of changes in that understanding. It is a vast theme on which whole libraries have been written, and I am conscious that I can do no more than scratch the surface of other people's thoughts. But it is also too important a theme to be left to intellectual specialists, because it touches ordinary life at many highly significant points. My aim, therefore, is to try to interpret a little of this vast mass of material from a Christian perspective, and to see how it might help us in facing some difficult contemporary moral issues. I have begun with these four markers simply to illustrate the kind of changes which have taken place in the last century and a half.

Nobody could pretend that Lewis Carroll actually influenced philosophy, despite the remark about him quoted earlier. Interest in Kafka seems to have reached a peak in Britain shortly after the Second World War, but the usual reaction to him has been bafflement. The experience of totalitarianism certainly changed perceptions of the dignity and value of human life, but mainly by reaction against it. It is impossible, for instance, to have a serious consideration of eugenics or euthanasia nowadays without some reference back to Nazi atrocities. Postmodernism is alive and well in the Sunday newspaper supplements, but outside fairly restricted intellectual circles, it is more a mood of individual self-assertion than a serious philosophical movement. All four points detailed above may seem marginal to the life of most ordinary people today. As markers, however, they may serve to illustrate some of the directions in which Western culture has been moving, and the importance of trying to find a more satisfying answer to Alice's question, 'Who in the world am I?'

The simplest and commonest answer is that each of

us is a person, and that as such we have a certain status, dignity and worth, which entail certain rights and obligations. Many other descriptions are possible, but the word 'person' has come to be the word which most fully expresses what has traditionally been felt to be most characteristic about ourselves. It is normal to distinguish sharply between persons and things. Most people hesitate to describe animals in personal terms, unless as a deliberate exaggeration or in an attempt to make a point about their intelligence. There are disputes about whether a highly intelligent computer should ever be described as a person. The ascription of personhood in our society carries with it an automatic moral status. If embryos, for instance, are properly to be defined as persons, then there should be no question about their right to full protection by the law.

Questions about who or what are persons are not only important, therefore, for our own self-understanding, but have a major impact on ethics and on public policy. I shall argue that the threat of meaninglessness and the devaluation of persons are part of the same intellectual, moral and social processes of change which have encouraged many people to see religion as meaningless and have for them devalued the idea of God. There is no simple way of reversing this process because the assumptions, perceptions and feelings which have driven it are now deeply embedded in our whole way of life. But to identify what has been happening and to provide alternative ways of thinking is at least to make a start. That is the purpose of this book.

There are, of course, other words we use to describe ourselves – human beings, men and women, individuals, selves, bodies and souls – all of which carry slightly different nuances of meaning. Like the word 'person', they can all carry moral weight when used in appropriate circumstances. I recall a dreadful television documentary on the death penalty, which showed a prisoner undergoing a botched execution, and shouting out, 'I am a human being ... I am a human being ...' What he was claiming was no different from what he might have claimed by saying, 'I am a person.' The nuances of language do not fit the neat categories we might like to prescribe for them. For the purpose of this book, however, I am going to concentrate on the word 'person' as the word most frequently used to convey a sense of value. I am content to leave open the question of whether other descriptions might be equally weighty.

I turn first to a tragic case which raised in its most acute form the question of where personhood begins and ends, and which can help to expose some of its many strands of meaning.

2

Between life and death

The Hillsborough disaster of 1989 is still very much part of public consciousness. It was one of those tragedies which sicken a nation, involving as it did the needless deaths of so many young people who had come together for an afternoon's enjoyment. It was to change the face of British football grounds.

A few days after it happened, I visited the Hillsborough ground and met some of those involved. The place was filled with what have now become familiar symbols after tragedies of this kind – innumerable bunches of flowers, football scarves and caps, personal messages and memorabilia. The scene was repeated on a much larger scale shortly afterwards at the Anfield ground in Liverpool, since this was where the majority of those killed had come from. Anfield became the scene of an extraordinary quasi-religious ritual which developed spontaneously without any formal planning. In the course of a week a million people filed through the ground, twice the population of the city. They queued for hours to get in. What started with a few people laying flowers became a tidal wave of symbolism, a community expression of grief embodied in gifts and acts of respect, an unforgettable experience of togetherness.

After leaving the Hillsborough ground I went to the Sheffield hospital where some of the victims had been taken, and vividly remember being taken into a private room where a boy was lying in a coma. Like the football pitches, this room was decorated with scarves, caps, football shirts, and all the personal mementos of a keen supporter, as if to say: 'Here are the things which matter to you; here is your world to wake up to' – for possessions can help to define our identity. I never discovered his name, but I am almost certain it was Tony Bland. And, of course, he never did wake up.

Some two and a half years later, I was badgered by the local media to comment on the request from Tony Bland's parents that he be allowed to die. It was a request supported by his doctor, but the local coroner had warned of the possibility of prosecution for murder if the request was carried out. My reply at that stage was that the law had to be obeyed, but that it should be possible for the parents to begin to detach themselves emotionally from what remained of Tony Bland. He had by then been diagnosed as being in a Persistent Vegetative State (PVS), and his doctors were convinced that there was no hope of recovery. I suggested that it was no longer necessary for his parents to visit him every day, as they had been doing, and that it might help them to begin to think of him as, for most practical purposes, already dead. This advice was indignantly rejected. In retrospect I think the parents were right. It is immensely difficult to change our emotional attachments simply by deciding to do so. The rituals of death are themselves evidence that something definitive has to happen before the emotional acceptance of it becomes possible.

A year later I found myself a member of the Select Committee of the House of Lords set up to look at the issues surrounding euthanasia, and in particular to review the Bland case and the significance of PVS. One of the members of the committee was a Lord of Appeal who, with three other judges, had decided at the end of a long legal process that it was permissible to withdraw feeding, and thus allow Tony Bland to starve to death. He gave us valuable insight into the finely balanced issues which had to be decided by the judges, and the many unanswered questions which remained. He was clearly troubled.

The Select Committee, which had already agreed that it was permissible to withdraw treatment in cases of terminal illness where there was no hope of improvement, was deeply divided on the issue of whether the withdrawal of feeding could rightly be classified as the withdrawal of treatment. The fact that food had to be given by artificial means, in this instance by stomach tube, satisfied the doctors that it was indeed a form of treatment. Other members of the committee, and particularly the nurses who gave evidence to us, tended to be uncomfortable at this suggestion. For them, in their daily contacts with patients, feeding was the minimum basic care owed to anybody who still had some semblance of life, however rudimentary.

That in bare outline is the story, a deeply disturbing

one in which I felt some personal sense of responsibility. It seems to me to raise most of the difficult questions about what we mean by a human 'person', why persons are valuable, and where we should draw the line between life and death. These are inescapable questions, not only for those who shape public policy, but for philosophers, scientists and theologians, who may misapprehend them, and falsify the nature of the issues if they ignore each other's disciplines. Questions about the nature and value of persons simply will not fit into our different academic compartments, and that is one reason why they are so difficult to handle. A concrete case, therefore, can help to focus our attention on the many dimensions and aspects involved.

Tony Bland was undoubtedly alive, and he was undoubtedly human. Nobody suggested that he should simply be dealt with as if he were already dead. He could breathe by himself. His limbs could move by themselves. He looked like the boy he had once been, but he was unresponsive to any sort of personal contact. Since his case was decided, there have been doubts in some other cases about the reliability of the PVS diagnosis. It was known in Tony Bland's case, however, that his cerebral cortex had been destroyed; in fact it had turned to liquid. So in what sense is someone without a cerebral cortex still to be regarded as a person? If he is not a person, what in the world is he?

Boundaries at the beginning of life

It is a question which arises, of course, at the other end of life as well. In what sense is an anencephalic infant, an infant without a brain, a person? What degree of personhood does an embryo have before the development of its central nervous system? The language used to discuss such issues is frequently rather slippery. An embryo is human, we are told, and it is alive, like Tony Bland, and therefore it deserves to be treated as a human being. But there is a difference between being human and being a human being. Transplanted human tissues are human and they are alive, but they are not human beings. To use the phrase 'a human being' implies a kind of organised wholeness, an identity, an individuality, a higher order of being than that of a single human organ. So the question becomes: how complete does a human being have to be in order to qualify morally as a person? This is a highly sensitive matter, not least for people with certain extreme forms of disability. It lies at the heart of the debate about abortion, and the use of embryos for research, and the disposal of frozen embryos. In the end it is not going to be answered in terms of anatomy and physiology; but scientific insights can hardly be irrelevant to the mapping of some of the boundaries.

There are those who argue, for instance, that our fundamental identity is genetic. Once a new genetic identity has been formed through the process of conception, there exists a potential new person with the same moral value as a fully developed person. A physiological event, in other words, marks the beginning of personhood. New genes equal new person. The equation has familiar consequences for moral beliefs about abortion and embryo research. It entails that the cut-off point, the boundary, for any potentially destructive interference is the moment of fertilisation. It also has some less widely noted implications for future work in genetics. If new genes really do equal new person, does it follow that the genes themselves should be as inviolate as the person into which they may develop? These are issues to which I shall be returning in Chapter 12. I mention them now as reminders of what hangs on apparently abstruse questions about the definition of personhood.

Another boundary, this time a legally prescribed one, disallows abortion beyond the age of twenty-four weeks, except in emergencies where the mother's life is endangered. This is roughly the age at which, according to some recent evidence, a fetus can not only feel pain, but may also be able to hear and smell. The main reason for fixing the limit at twenty-four weeks, however, is that beyond this age a fetus stands a good chance of being viable on its own. Twenty-four weeks thus marks a boundary, though not a legal one, between abortion and infanticide, and implies a criterion of personhood relating to the possibility of independent existence. A person, according to this definition, has to be capable of separate individual life, and viability is the boundary at which such separation and individuality become possible. But it is not a clear or fixed boundary because it is in practice determined by the current state of medical skill. Arguments about the abortion of deformed fetuses are ostensibly about the quality of life such a fetus might expect, but the quality of life criterion in fact tends to be assessed in large measure in terms of the possibility of independent existence. A human being totally dependent on others for all natural functions, so the argument goes, has little chance of developing the qualities normally associated with personhood. Individuality and independence are by no means the same, but there is a relationship between them which underlies perceptions about what it is to be a person.

Being is belonging

In the case of Tony Bland, we find a form of disablement so complete that although he had an individual existence, he had no independence to do anything beyond the mere fact of existing. All he seemed to retain of his former personhood was his genetic identity and continuing bodily presence.

This is not the way his parents and friends originally saw him. The fact that his room was hung with symbols of football was a reminder to them and to others that his life was lived in a particular cultural context. Personhood is not some sort of abstract quality which exists in a vacuum. We are what we are because of the things we have experienced, the language we speak, the people to whom we relate, the possessions we value, and these are all part of a larger cultural environment which shapes the way our personhood expresses itself.

I recently came across the following passage in a Korean guidebook:

Once you have tried to jostle your way through the rush-hour crowds of downtown Seoul and been buffetted from pillar to post by what seems like every third person without any murmur of apology, you might get the impression that Koreans are a rude bunch. The truth lies elsewhere and is to be found in the Confucian education system which lacks a code of behaviour for relating to outsiders. You simply don't fit into any traditional category so many Koreans have difficulty relating to you as they can't place you.

This is only one among countless examples of how fundamental aspects of consciousness are conditioned by culture. For Confucian-orientated Koreans, the acknowledgment of another person's identity depends on social markers without which relationships cannot be formed. Likewise Tony Bland's scarf and cap and other possessions signalled his continuing place within a particular culture, and the thousands of memorabilia at Anfield were an expression of the corporate consciousness of Liverpool fans, and a reaffirmation of their identity.

Cultural identity by itself, however, is only a very weak marker of continuing personal identity, though there are circumstances in which it can be crucial. One of the most effective ways of disorientating, demoralising and eventually depersonalising people is to strip them of all that makes life familiar and secure, techniques used with devastating effect on many of the victims of totalitarianism. In death, when so much of what constitutes a person seems lost for ever, graves and memorabilia can express a minimal kind of continuing social role. In some parts of Eastern Europe Orthodox Christians believe that the soul does not leave the body until the latter has decomposed. The body is therefore exhumed after several years, the bones washed, then finally laid to rest. In other Christian traditions the doctrine of purgatory, and of the communion of saints, can maintain a strong awareness of the abiding presence of the dead. In less religious contexts the cultural dimension of personal identity is sustained after death only in the memory of friends and relatives. For some that is the only concept of survival, which may be one reason why so many people long to have an heir, or to do something memorable, so that it can be said of them, 'They lived; they died; they made a difference.'

What is missing, of course, in the situations I have been describing, is communication, all that we associate with language in the development and sustenance of human personality. The crucial fact about Tony Bland, which led to doubts about his continuing personhood, was the total absence of meaningful communication. Such communication does not have to be through the spoken or written word. Stories of massively disabled patients who communicate by blinking an eyelid or waggling a toe show that there can be a rich mental life even when other forms of communication are almost wholly frustrated. The bestselling autobiography of one such victim, a French journalist, revealed an amazingly perceptive mind locked into an almost totally unresponsive body. Such cases raise the question of whether there might still be a mental life when there is no communication at all. I shall return to this problem later. Meanwhile, the point at issue is that personhood, as we normally understand it, is shaped by and depends on communication, and in cases where there has never been meaningful linguistic communication the personality remains unformed.

Austin Farrer had a delightful sermon in which he compared human beings to moles, which apparently need to eat every few minutes if they are to survive. 'Our souls like the poor mole's body, die away when they have no humanity to feed upon . . . The trouble is, that if we are always enjoying our friends by the direct method, we suck them, and they suck us, dry.' He then refers to reading or praying as alternative ways of relating to other people's minds, and goes on, 'But whether reading, talking or praying, we get our mouth full of mankind; and mankind is our proper food.' Why? Because this kind of relatedness, this mutual feeding upon one another, has not only been blessed by God, so that communion is at the very heart of our being, but is an expression of the life of God himself in the mutuality of Father, Son and Holy Spirit. Theology is always lurking on the edge of language about relatedness. Such a claim does not, of course, prove anything. I mention it at this stage simply to indicate an area of common interest.

Tony Bland's parents still related to him, and reacted indignantly to my suggestion that they might properly and appropriately begin to relate less closely. What were they relating to? A well-loved body? A set of memories? A hope? Perhaps all these things. But they did not feel able to release themselves from the commitment to be there with him, and to relate to whatever he still was, until something had happened which they could clearly recognise as death.

What might this be? Stoppage of the heart has traditionally been regarded as the main criterion of death. Resuscitation techniques and transplant surgery have changed the picture medically, but it is still difficult for many people to accept that a patient may be dead, even though the heart is still beating. Emotional problems with so-called 'beating heart organ donors', kept going by artificial respiration, reflect millennia of belief that where there is a beating heart there is still life.

The other traditional indicator of death, the cessation of respiration, provides a clearer basis for diagnosing death, in so far as it implies that the brain stem is no longer functioning. The definition of brain death, which paved the way for transplant surgery, specifies the cessation of electrical activity in the brain stem, the implication being that if the brain stem is non-functional then the cerebral cortex must be non-functional also. In such patients, switching off the respirator is done in recognition of the fact that death has already occurred, but as breathing and circulation will have been maintained, organs for transplantation can be removed in good condition. In a case of PVS, however, the brain stem is not dead, so nobody really knows what this might mean in terms of some rudimentary form of consciousness or feeling. If there is something there which can still feel, is that something the person – frustrated perhaps by an inability to communicate? Or is it just the debris of the person, a few mental left-overs? Or is it no more than a body which continues its unconscious bodily functions, most of which never impinge on awareness in normal people unless something goes wrong with them?

This brings us to the subject of consciousness on which, again, I shall have more to say later. For the moment it is enough to note that there are degrees of consciousness. Many, perhaps most, animals have consciousness of a kind, and in animals with which we are familiar we can see this reaching quite sophisticated levels. I got into trouble a few years ago when speculating that some of the higher apes might have a degree of consciousness approaching our own, and earned the immortal headline in the *Daily Mail*: 'Apes have souls, says Primate'. Dog and cat owners know that their pets can plan strategies, use persuasion, and demonstrate their feelings. Dogs appear to have dreams, and must presumably therefore experience some conscious life independent of immediate sensory awareness, but only the most sentimental would suggest that they have anything approaching human self-awareness. On this analogy there is nothing intrinsically absurd in imagining a quasi-conscious state for humans, in which the most distinctive human capacities are lost but some residual, animal-like consciousness remains. It is impossible for us to know what such residual consciousness would be like, though it would presumably involve at the very least some kind of sentience and emotional capacity. But this is speculation. On the whole I think the odds are against there being any brain-stem consciousness at all without the survival of at least part of the cortex.

Internal and external attributes

If I am right in this, then it would be fair to say that Tony Bland had lost almost all the attributes through which persons normally relate to one another – consciousness, self-awareness and the ability to communicate. But he had retained some of the outward markers of personhood – bodily continuity, physical signs of life, a minimal degree of responsiveness to stimulation, a history symbolised by his treasured possessions, and by his still active role in the lives of those caring for him. Within his family there was a gradually attenuating sense of relationship which needed some decisive terminating action to enable them to let go. His dependence on them and on those who cared for him came to be seen as no more than a one-sided physical dependence, and eventually this was no longer enough. Roughly, the distinction here is between what we might call the inward attributes of personhood, entailing some kind of communication, and the external attributes, located in a particular physical history.

Suppose we read back this distinction into the deep disagreements on the subject of embryos. Those who would disallow any interference from the moment of conception onwards are implying that the physical, historical indicators of personhood are important enough to carry the full moral weight ascribed to complete persons. The embryo, in this view, may only represent the first page of a story, but it is a continuous story whose beginning is just as important as its end. Those who take a less absolutist view of abortion are implying that physical continuity is not by itself a sufficient indicator of personhood. In this view the moral weight of personhood rests on inward attributes which enable us to be aware of ourselves and to relate to others, attributes which cannot even have the semblance of a beginning until there is at least a rudimentary nervous system, and until some actual relationship is in process of formation. The stage at which an expectant mother begins to relate consciously to the fetus in her womb no doubt varies greatly with individuals, but the first consciously felt movements have always been a significant landmark; this is why quickening was traditionally regarded as the point beyond which abortion was forbidden. To lay the emphasis on these internal attributes need not entail treating the external physical attributes, which develop earlier, as insignificant. It is a matter of degree, of the possibilities of personhood, and hence of the moral weight to be put in the balance against any considerations in favour of interference or termination.

Process rather than event

Just as this latter kind of thinking has encouraged the view that the development of personhood is a slow, multi-dimensional process, so cases like that of Tony Bland force us to think in similar terms about the meaning of death. In the light of such cases, it may be necessary to regard death also as often more of a gradual process than as a precisely timed event. There are obvious difficulties for some forms of Christian thinking in this emphasis on process, particularly when the soul is regarded as a separate entity which a person does or does not possess. A kind of gradualism does make sense when one is watching the slow dissolution of a person through illness or old age, even though it is hard to let go of the idea that there has to be a particular moment we call death. Transplant surgery has led to a more general acceptance that different parts of the body may die at different times, but there is something about the unity of the person which seems to be crucial in defining death itself, and it may be that when we talk about the soul it is this unity we are trying to describe. Uncertainty about where, if anywhere, such unity resides lies at the heart of our agonising over PVS and similar conditions.

In mainline Western philosophy the unity of the person has been seen as internal and inescapably linked with self-awareness. Just as in a drawing the lines of perspective extend back to focus on a point where the observer's eye is assumed to be, so for centuries it has been assumed that the self is like an invisible point at the focus of all our experience. But there are difficulties. Some of these have been apparent ever since psychiatrists began the clinical study of multiple personalities. Other worries are more common and more widely distributed. Not everybody nowadays feels that they are a united self. In fact, one of the disturbing features of modern Western consciousness is the sense of fragmentation, the awareness of playing many roles, and deep uncertainties about who or what one is. We know, as previous generations did not, to what great extent the self is a social construction, the product of our interactions with countless other people, shaped by the social conventions of our day. Recall the Koreans and their supposed inability to relate to foreigners. Many of those who have seriously absorbed such insights tend to be beset by haunting fears that this is all, that there is nothing at the centre, that the focal point is simply the place, without content, where all the lines cross.

Despite the sense of fragmentation, however, and actual fragmentation in a few cases, most people do display a consistency of character, even if it is a consistency in being disorganised. Perhaps it is precisely in this ability to handle a multiplicity of influences that the uniqueness of persons resides. Unless things go seriously wrong, most people have the extraordinary capacity to weave many strands together and produce out of them a more or less coherent set of responses which they call 'being myself'. This is an active process. Their unity and identity as persons may be rooted in biology and shaped by culture, but they do not behave as if they were mere passive recipients, pushed around by the sum total of the influences on them. The unity and identity of personhood seem to be created in the process of responding to multifarious experiences on the basis of more or less consistent intentions and dispositions. We can call the process 'soul-making', but I prefer the expression 'person-making'. The problem with the word 'soul' is that it carries such strong implications of something distinct and separable from the whole person. It also has an all-or-nothing quality about it which does not fit the picture of gradual development and the possibility of gradual loss, which I have been trying to describe. Personhood is not just a quality, or set of qualities, given to us. It is a state of being rooted in, and developing through, mutual interaction with other persons. On the question of how unity and identity arise out of this interaction, I shall have more to say later. All the themes opened up in this chapter will recur in various guises.

There I shall leave it for now. I have used the tragic case of Tony Bland to tease out some of the complex questions which have to be asked about someone surviving at the very borders of personal existence. I have been concerned to stress the many levels on which one needs to think about personhood, and I have begun to spell out some of the implications of adopting a gradualist approach. It is now time to look much more directly at the way present concepts of personhood have evolved, and in particular at the major contribution of Christian theology to their development. We shall then be better placed to return to some of the practical issues which are vitally affected by the way we understand ourselves.

3

A surfeit of meanings

An old psychology textbook with the title *Personality* starts by listing fifty different definitions of the word 'person'. So many meanings have been poured into the word that discussion of whether, and in what sense, Tony Bland was still a person, could become vacuous without some attempt to limit them. Nor is it only in acute circumstances like his that differences of understanding affect the way people feel and behave. Assumptions about what persons are undergird our whole way of life, and if these change, then in the long run our moral beliefs and attitudes change too. In this and the following chapter, therefore, I intend to give a brief history of the word as a preliminary to looking more closely at what it is we are valuing when we say that persons matter.

It is difficult to think ourselves back into a world where the concept of 'person', as we now use it, did not exist. Anthropologists describe forms of tribal life in which community consciousness is so strong that there is little sense of individual identity. The self spills over into other people, to such an extent that outside the tribe existence is not only dangerous but meaningless. The fluidity of the boundaries between people is particularly obvious in the work of traditional healers, even in relatively modernised African societies. It is taken for granted that one person's thoughts and feelings can flow into someone else, for good or ill. Everything, as far as such people are concerned, depends on relationships. Sickness is a sign that a relationship has gone wrong, that from one side or the other evil has been intended, and needs to be exposed by confronting the guilty party, before healing can take place.

The same is true of politics. In the new South Africa the Truth and Reconciliation Commission was based on the premise, fundamental to African thinking, that the restoration of right relationships is a crucial step in the righting of wrongs. The administration of justice may have to follow, but truth and reconciliation are primary, because a failure in reconciliation wounds everybody, including those who carry the grievances.

This strong sense of inter-relationship is a far cry from the modern Western concept of autonomous individuals, increasingly concerned to manage their own lives and illnesses, and eager to jump into litigation to secure their rights against others. It is the main theme of this book that somewhere between these extremes of total mutual involvement or atomised independence, the word 'person' points to a richer and more complex way of being human.

Greece and Rome

The ancient civilisations known best within European culture, those of Greece and Rome, are in many ways so familiar, and form so much of our Western heritage, that we are apt to think of their understanding of persons as very like our own. But though they had the words – *persona* in Latin, and *prosopon* in Greek – the meanings were different. Both were used primarily to refer to an actor's mask, a role, an appearance, rather than to what a human being essentially is.

Both cultures were dominated by a strong sense of order. Indeed, to feel at home in any culture is to interpret it as part of a given order. Among twentieth-century intelligentsia the type of order most strongly perceived and valued has to a large extent been shaped by science and mathematics. Ancient Greek thought likewise emphasised the unity and mathematical harmony of nature, but unlike today this was held to include the moral and social order. In fact, the cosmic scheme of things was so all-embracing that it was difficult to find a philosophical place in it for free, independent individuals. Human beings, according to Plato, existed for the sake of the whole. It was only in the theatre, behind the masks, that the order could be challenged by reworking the ancient myths.

Thus it was that a free spirit like Antigone could act out her role in defiance of the fates. Whether Sophocles was really asserting the independence of a free spirit in anything like the modern sense is debatable, but the play itself has proved to be timeless and endlessly fertile. Antigone's story is on one level the classic expression of conflict between the state and individual conscience. She feels impelled to bury her dead brother in defiance of King Creon's edict that the bodies of traitors must be left to rot where they are. She appeals to the laws of the gods against what she sees as mere human intransigence, while Creon insists that his decision to abide by what he has decreed is essential for social stability. The inevitable tragedy unfolds in dialogue of enormous depth and subtlety. The masked figures on stage are not individuals as they might be understood today, however. They are more like poetic symbols, rooted in the myths of the past, and acting out the tragic consequences of an ultimately incomprehensible fate. Nor is the conflict quite what it seems to modern eyes. When at the end Antigone finally reveals her motive for disobeying Creon's command, it turns out to be not so much an assertion of individual conscience against the state as a simple expression of family solidarity within the doomed House of Oedipus. In her final speech as she is led away to die, she declares that she would not have defied Creon for a husband or a son, because she could always have replaced these; but where could she find another brother? Thus even the classic archetype of the rebellious individual sees herself in the end as part of a larger family whole.

This same consciousness of a given order of things was true of the Romans, but they, with their emphasis on law, were less concerned with cosmic roles than with social ones. They developed the word for the actor's mask (*per sona* – literally what the actor 'spoke through') to include the role someone plays in life.

From there it came to represent the qualities needed to fulfil that role. By the time of Cicero (106–43 BC) *persona* had four strands of meaning:

1 Appearance, as in the theatre, a meaning which has returned with a vengeance in our modern obsession with a person's public image.
2 Role or status, as in professional or social life. This carried the implication that a role also entails a given pattern of relationships, and belongs within a certain social order.
3 The attributes required by a role. It is in this third meaning that we find the beginnings of the use of the word as applied to the inner self.
4 Dignity and prerogative, a meaning which eventually crystallised around the word 'personage' and also contains the idea of the free person, or citizen, as well as the representative person, or 'parson'. In Roman law slaves were not persons, a belief which proved immensely hard to eradicate, despite later Christian assertions that everybody, slave or free, had the same personal value in the sight of God.

'Person' in biblical thought

The four Ciceronian meanings lie at the root of most subsequent developments. There are echoes of the second and fourth in the New Testament when St Paul, in trying to defend himself against fellow Jews who were threatening his life, appeals not to Jewish law, but to his Roman citizenship. His security, in other words, lay in his role within the Roman order of things, which gave him both dignity and protection. Admittedly he was also aware of a deeper security which he described as being 'in Christ', and this might be seen as a combination of meanings one and three. First it is necessary to 'put on Christ', using the metaphor of clothing, as an actor might be clothed and masked for a particular role. Thereafter the Christian imperative is to 'become what you are', in other words, so to enact the role as to internalise this new relationship with Christ, until it becomes the reality undergirding the Christian's life.

The seeds were already present, therefore, from which new Christian understandings of the Latin word *persona* could grow. In the Bible itself the concept did not receive much attention. The word carried no particular overtones until it was taken up into Christian theology. In the Old Testament people are described primarily in terms of action and character; they do 'good or evil in the sight of the Lord', and there is frequently no explanation of what motivates them, as when Pharaoh's heart is inexplicably hardened in response to Moses' request to let his people go. The focus of attention throughout most of the Old Testament is on the story of divine initiative in which human beings play their allotted roles, rather than on the inner turmoils of individuals. There is a strong sense of tribal and family solidarity, which makes it seem not unreasonable that God should 'punish the children for the sins of the parents to the third and fourth generation' – a phrase in the Ten Commandments which is conveniently forgotten in most contemporary appeals to restore them as the basis of moral teaching. It is only in the later prophetic books, especially Jeremiah and Ezekiel, that the sense of individual responsibility becomes more prominent, and there is increasing emphasis on the personal internalisation of morality. Jeremiah's famous complaints against God, as in chapter 15, verses 15–18, together with many of the Psalms and in the book of Job, are examples of this new emphasis.

In the New Testament it is predominant, with many references to good and evil being located in the 'heart'. The teaching of Jesus about the importance of individuals, particularly the weakest and most despised, echoes the same theme. But this is in no sense a commendation of individualism; people matter as individuals because they belong together as children of the one heavenly Father. The word *prosopon*, in so far as it is used at all, almost always carries its primary meaning of 'face' or 'appearance', and there is only one reference (2 Cor. 1:11) where it seems to mean people as such. In general, therefore, it is fair to say that the broad thrust of the Bible is neither to regard people as puppets in the hands of fate, like the characters in Greek dramas, nor to treat them in the modern fashion as autonomous individuals. People are known in their relationship to God and to one another. Their vocation is to respond to God in the outworking of his moral purposes.

Persons of the Trinity

It was under the impetus of the doctrinal disputes during the first few Christian centuries that the concept of 'person' received a huge injection of theological meaning. It is a long, complex story, centring on the doctrines of the Trinity and of the Person of Christ, and the struggle to find acceptable ways of saying what had never been said before. Trinitarian theology had somehow to express both unity and diversity within the nature of God. The unity was essential because the legacy of Jewish faith had made the idea of multiple gods inconceivable. God is either the sole source and ground of all that is, or he is not God. But God had also revealed himself in Jesus Christ, who was perceived and worshipped as the only valid image of God, and witnessed to internally by the Holy Spirit as a source of power and enlightenment within. The issue was set out at its starkest in the baptismal formula at the end of St Matthew's Gospel, where the disciples of Jesus are told to baptise 'in the name of the Father, and of the Son, and of the Holy Spirit'.

One of the difficulties in trying to express both threeness and oneness in a less symbolic and more philosophical fashion lay in finding terms which were not already loaded with unwanted meanings. It was compounded by the need to reach agreement in both Greek and Latin. The eventual formulation that God is 'three persons in one substance' was the result of centuries of argument and misunderstanding. As we have seen, the word 'person' in Latin carries the primary meaning of 'role'. Thus to describe God as 'three persons' might seem to reduce the threeness of God to three aspects or modes, as if God first showed one face to humanity, then another, with the distinctions between them appearing to be only temporary and superficial. Indeed, when one of the early Latin theologians, Tertullian (AD 160–225), first suggested the use of 'person', he seems to have had in mind the analogy of the *dramatis personae* in a play, possibly as in Psalm 2, itself a kind of drama in which God decrees, 'You are my son, today I have begotten you.' The difficulty with the dramatic analogy is that if Father, Son and Spirit are merely descriptions of the One God acting out different roles, and are not in some sense really distinct, how is it possible to understand the work of Jesus in bringing us to the Father, and in sending us the Spirit? The concept of 'role' is too weak to carry the belief that something new and vital had actually been achieved in terms of humanity's relation to God, by the living, dying and rising of Jesus.

The Greek theologians spared themselves this problem by avoiding the use of their word *prosopon* to describe the threeness. They preferred *hypostasis*, which has a much stronger meaning and signifies real, concrete existence. The word is derived from the notion of dregs, the solid stuff at the bottom of a liquid, that which 'stands underneath'. Unfortunately, its Latin equivalent is the word *substantia* (also meaning 'standing underneath'), which the Latin theologians had already used for their description of the underlying unity of God. Meanwhile, the Greeks referred to this underlying unity as *ousia*, or 'being', a derivative of 'to be', a word hardly distinguishable in meaning from *hypostasis*, as it too implies real, concrete existence. To talk of three *hypostases* in one *ousia* could thus have given the impression that the Greek theologians believed in three Gods. They avoided this by distinguishing what is common to the Godhead, *ousia*, from what is particular to the *hypostases*, their interrelationships. The key differentiation within the Godhead was thus expressed in terms of relationships. All that God does is *from* the Father, *through* the Son and *in* the Spirit. If all this seems a bit mind-boggling, it is worth recalling the standard formula for Christian prayer, which follows precisely this pattern. Christians pray *to* the Father, *through* the Son and *in* the Spirit, and prayer is essentially about being caught up into this relationship with the One God. C.S. Lewis once described it vividly as a kind of heavenly dance.

Given these differences of approach, language and terminology between theologians who were isolated from one another in the eastern and western halves of the Roman Empire, it is not surprising that they found it hard to understand one another, and still harder to agree.

Agreement that three *personae* in one *substantia* meant the same as three *hypostases* in one *ousia* only became possible as the word *persona* began to take on some of the meaning of the word *hypostasis*. Thus the two notions of role and particular, concrete existence or being were brought together in a single term. To cut a very long story short, one result of this complex theological discussion was an immense enrichment of the language of personhood. What I referred to earlier as the third meaning of the original Latin word, namely the attributes needed to fulfil a role, could now include the idea of particular existence, and so pave the way for 'person' to refer to the innermost reality of a human being. Add to this the fact that the word still carried its reference to role and status, and hence implied inter-relationship with other persons; add, too, the fact that the same word now expressed inter-relationships within the being of God himself, and it is not hard to see the potential revolution in human self-understanding which began to open up. What to us may seem a remote, technical, theological discussion paved the way for a new kind of fusion between role and reality. To describe someone as a person no longer need imply that they were merely fulfilling a role, whether in a cosmic drama in Greece or as a citizen in Rome. It remained true that persons were what they were by virtue of the roles they played and the relationships in which they stood towards others, but the word now meant more than that. It pointed to a quality of being analogous to God's own being. Personhood, in other words, is about being real, as God is real.

There were equally stupendous implications in the complex controversies concerning the Person of Christ, centred on how it might be possible for a single person to be both human and divine. Since my main concern at this stage is not theological, but to sketch briefly how the word 'person' came to acquire its range of meanings, I simply note that here again it acted as a linking concept between humanity and divinity. Implicit in the notion of incarnation is the belief that humanity can in some sense bear the image of the divine, a belief which, when taken seriously, entails a revolution in the understanding of human possibilities.

In the event, neither revolution progressed immediately very far. Abstract theology is one thing and life is another, and it took centuries for the implications of this kind of thinking to seep through into ordinary consciousness – in so far as they ever have. The story continues to be one of false starts and blind alleys, and it is only in quite recent years that the full potential of trinitarian theology has once again come to the fore as a possible source of self-understanding. Books on the Trinity pour from the theological presses. A favourite theme is that just as the Persons of the Trinity are essentially related to one another, so human personality is essentially a relational term. We are what we are in communion with others. It is an attractive interpretation in an age when there is a felt need to restore a stronger sense of community, but it is important to remember the complex background from which it comes. I shall be returning to this theme in Chapters 8 and 10.

The actual history of the word 'person' took a different course. Its trinitarian implications, in terms of our own inter-relatedness and substantial reality, failed to be developed. The result has been a certain impoverishment, the full significance of which is only now becoming clear in the light of modern threats to the very idea of personhood.

The image of God

Before turning to this history, however, I need to make a detour back to the Bible, to pick up an obvious point about the link between belief in God and belief in personhood. I have been arguing that the link was potentially strengthened and enriched at the time when classic Christian doctrine was being formulated. Its origins lie much deeper. In fact, the intimate relationship between beliefs about God and beliefs about man is set out quite explicitly in the first chapter of Genesis. 'God created man in his own image, in the image of God he created him; male and female he created them' (Gen. 1:27). Precisely how this is to be interpreted has been the subject of endless debate. Nevertheless, it has been a key text in Jewish and Christian thinking about the nature of humanity, and for Christians it found fulfilment in the belief in Jesus as the only true and complete image of God.

It has also been the focus of one of the most common objections to all I have been saying so far about the Godward thrust of this word 'person'. Not much imagination is needed to turn the text on its head, and proclaim, as many have done throughout the centuries, that God is made in the image of man. Far from discovering the depths of our own personhood in the personhood of God, says the sceptic, we merely project our consciousness of personhood onto a blank screen set up by our own fears and longings. It is an objection which probably even pre-dates the Genesis text, and the first recorded example of it is in the writings of the sixth-century BC Greek philosopher Xenophanes: 'The lions if they could have pictured God would have pictured him in fashion like a lion . . .' He, however, was probably not using it as a sceptical argument, but as a reminder of the limitations of human thought. Rupert Brooke was to do the same two and a half millennia later in his famous poem on the fish's idea of heaven, which in 1995 struck such a chord that it came second in the poetry popularity stakes.

> And there they trust there swimmeth one
> Who swam ere rivers were begun,
> Immense, of fishy form and mind
> Squamous, omnipotent and kind . . .

It concludes with the immortal lines

> And in that heaven of all their wish,
> There shall be no more land, say fish.
>
> ['Heaven', 1915]

So in the end it all comes down to wish-fulfilment. Brooke, and the thousands of present-day sceptics who have deployed the same argument, have sharper weapons than Xenophanes. Some are derived from more sophisticated psychological theories of mental projection, and some are the work of upside-down theologians like Feuerbach, and more recently Don Cupitt and his disciples, who have tried to interpret the whole of theology as if it has no reference outside purely human experience. God is a powerful human idea, not in any sense an objective reality. Theology, in other words, is anthropology with knobs on.

We get closer to the truth, I believe, if we describe the process of forming ideas about God and about humanity in terms of interaction. This seems to have been what was happening in the story of trinitarian theology. Ideas about God and ideas about human personhood can be seen as developing together, each shaping and enriching the other. The late Austin Farrer in his book *The Glass of Vision* has a memorable paragraph describing a similar process in the growth of the idea of kingship:

> When human kings arose, invisible divine kings stood behind their thrones. Indeed kingship worthy of the name is distinguished from mere leadership by the divinity which supports it. Now if kings arose with divine support, we might suppose that the divine king was already known: for how can a human king be clothed with divine authority except by a divine king already acknowledged? But then on the other hand, until men have seen human kings, how can they know what a divine king would be? In fact, the human king and his divine archetype arise at once, they are inseparable: each makes the other.

This is a much more sophisticated way of understanding how religious concepts develop than the crude claim that theology is a mere reflection of anthropology. It makes sense of the progressive refinement of such concepts, and does justice to the real awareness of discovery which accompanies the process. The fact that it is a gradual and somewhat erratic process also explains why religion has to tolerate a certain amount of illusion as a necessary part of its exploration of that which no images can ultimately contain. There is an important difference between illusion and delusion. An illusion may offer a glimpse of understanding, a delusion none at all. A child paddling in the sea may be under the illusion that it now knows what the ocean is. But it would be deluded if it thought that it was actually standing on dry land. Those who believed that God could be found 'walking in the garden in the cool of the day' may have been under an illusion, but that does not mean that they were suffering a total delusion. For them it may have been a first step in discerning a personal presence. The next steps would have to entail the realisation that all such discernments are partial, potentially misleading, and have to be surpassed. This is the case even with such a seminal insight as that of man being made in the image of God.

God is not a large, invisible person. This is a concept of him which should have been dismissed millennia ago, but still persists, even if only at a jocular level. Winston Churchill, when dining once during the war with Lord Halifax and his wife, said with some emotion in the course of their conversation, 'That old man up there intended me to be where I am at this time.' The remark caused some confusion until Lady Halifax 'realised that he was talking about the Almighty and His Divine Providence and Purpose'. Churchill's theology was illusory, but in the light of events it is hard to think that he was wholly deluded. Beyond the illusion of 'that old man up there' lies the belief that

God is personal, that he is concerned with us and our destinies, and that there is that in him which relates to our own deepest understanding of ourselves. That way of putting it may itself be corrigible, but it is the fruit of a long process of discovery and criticism, in which it cannot be assumed that all the insights arose simply from wish-fulfilment and self-analysis.

To adapt Austin Farrer's analogy, we can ask whether it is true, for instance, that we human beings need some inkling of divine transcendence in order to shape and develop our own capacity for self-transcendence? What, in fact, could it mean to transcend ourselves without some concept, however vague, of that which is higher than ourselves? Again, while it is true that each of us develops as a person through our interaction with other persons, it is also true that we discern a oneness within ourselves; so it is reasonable to ask whether the sum of all these interactions itself represents some kind of over-arching unity external to us. How have we come to experience and value personal reality as supremely important, unless human beings have within themselves a kind of divine discontent towards all that would reduce us to being less than persons?

The name given to God in the Old Testament is itself profoundly suggestive: 'I AM THAT I AM'. God is self-evident, as our own existence is self-evident. The mystery of our existence, what philosophers have sometimes described as 'being', is an aspect and reflection of the mystery of all existence and its ground in 'Being' itself. This is not acceptable language to most philosophers nowadays, but it hints at something inescapably mysterious in the two simple words 'I

AM'. The self-description of God, as found in Exodus 3:14, can also be translated 'I WILL BE WHAT I WILL BE', the implication being that God reveals himself in human history. This too can be seen as going hand in hand with a process of human self-discovery. Putting these two meanings together, we find Moses being told that the reality he was discerning was outside him as well as within him, before him as well as beside him. The same logic works for idols as well. When the Psalmist said of these, 'They that make them are like unto them' (Psalm 115:8) he was expressing a caricature of the truth which confronted Moses. We become like what we worship.

None of this is a knock-down answer to the charge that, in believing in God, human beings merely project an ideal image of themselves. My concern in making this detour has been not so much to argue a case as to show that the process of forming concepts, whether of God or of ourselves, is much more complex and much more closely interwoven than those who put forward crude theories of projection commonly suppose. I shall return to the argument in Chapter 10. My immediate point is that, in this early history of the word 'person', there is no way in which the development of its meaning can be detached from theology.

Saint Augustine

This dependence on theology is especially obvious in the man who, perhaps more than any other, shaped Western Christian consciousness and gave new depth to the concept of intimate relationship with God. St Augustine (AD 354–430) is best known for his *Confessions*, an unparalleled exercise in religious and psychological self-exploration. The whole basis of his thinking is that he cannot truly be himself except in relationship with God, and as if to prove this the book itself is in the form of a dialogue with God. In Book X, para 8, for instance, he asks what he loves when he loves God, and he runs through a catalogue of delights of the senses:

> None of these I love, when I love my God; and yet I love a kind of light, and melody, and fragrance, and meat, and embracement, when I love my God, the light, melody, fragrance, meat, embracement of my inner man: where there shineth unto my soul, what space cannot contain, and there soundeth what time beareth not away, and there smelleth what breathing disperseth not, and there tasteth, what eating diminisheth not, and there clingeth what satiety divorceth not. This is it which I love, when I love my God.

How can we love what we do not know, a reality which utterly transcends us? Not by elevated aspirations; not just by loving other people; not even by loving Jesus as historically revealed to us. In the words of a great commentator on St Augustine: 'God must give his presence to the soul, both as the light that enlightens and as the fire that kindles; and knowledge and love must grow up together, mutually confirming one another. In other words, God himself is the condition of *all* human apprehension of him. We know him through his gifts, because his gift is of himself' (John Burnaby, *Amor Dei*, p. 143).

Augustine thus sees himself as utterly dependent on God for all that he is, including his knowledge of God. God says to him, as it were, 'You would not seek me, unless you had already found me.' But this seeking and finding has to take place in the depths of his being. What Augustine is doing, in fact, is to move the focus of religion inwards to the depths of his soul, to the point where God is already at work in him, and the restless heart finds its ultimate rest in the One who made it.

Later in Book X he explores the nature of memory (by which he seems to mean the whole mind, conscious and unconscious) in a marvellous feat of introspection, and is amazed at its seemingly unfathomable depths:

> Great is the power of memory, a fearful thing, O my God, a deep and boundless manifoldness; and this thing is the mind, and this am I myself . . . What shall I do then, O Thou my true life, my God? I will pass even beyond this power of mine which is called memory; yea I will pass beyond it . . . . See, I am mounting up through my mind towards Thee who abidest above me.

In other passages he speaks to God as 'thou light of my heart, thou bread of my soul, thou power who givest vigour to my mind, who quickenest my thoughts . . . Thou wert within, and I abroad, and there I searched for thee.'

Most explicitly of all, he counsels in one of his other writings, 'Do not go outward, return within yourself. In the inward man dwells truth.'

This profound sense of God as known inwardly is reflected in Augustine's interpretation of the Trinity. He saw dangers in too much emphasis on the separate Persons of the Godhead, and preferred to use the concept of personhood as applicable to the Trinity as a whole. He claimed that it is only possible to speak of the image of God in man because human personality is itself triune, and he used a series of analogies, none of them very convincing in modern eyes, to prove the point. Memory, intelligence and will, for example, can be thought of as separate components of personality, distinguished from one another by their inter-relationships, but unmistakably expressions of a single person. A better analogy, not so dependent on dubious psychology, is based on the three major terms used to describe God in St John's Gospel – Life, Light and Love. God as Life is the source and ground of all that is; as Light he is the one who has revealed himself in history, and supremely in the earthly life of Jesus; as Love he is the one who draws us to himself through his own self-giving. All three have their counterpart in human beings who live the life God has given them, can know in the light God has given them, and are enabled to love because they are first loved by him.

Augustine succeeded in showing to his contemporaries that the idea of threeness in oneness was not absurd. He also immeasurably deepened the concept of personality by linking it through his analogies to the internal being of God. He has been much criticised in recent years for his emphasis on inward reflection as the road to God, and for fixing Western theology in a mould which was to lead eventually to self-obsessed individualism. The personality explored in such depth, say these critics, is an isolated personality, not the person in relation with others, characteristic of Eastern trinitarian theology. I am not sure the criticisms are wholly deserved, and it would be strange if someone whose whole theology proclaimed the truth that love is nothing if it is not shared, could be accused of not placing enough emphasis on relatedness. Augustine was also well aware that his introspection carried the danger of self-deception, and that is why it was always set in the context of God's revelation through Scripture. Nor was it purely individual. He saw his own story as a microcosm of the story of creation, the exposition of which forms the last three books of the *Confessions.* Most striking of all is his theology of the sacraments, which for him were anchor points rescuing believers from subjectivity.

It was Augustine who taught the Church that the sacraments were used as instruments by God, even when administered by unworthy people, and even when they had no immediate effect in the lives of those who received them. His contribution to sacramental theology has been summed up by the Roman Catholic theologian, Bernard Leeming, in these words:

The Christian world has reason to be grateful to St Augustine. He asserted a principle of stability and security which applied in the diocese, parish, and the home. Amid the vagaries of human sinfulness and of perverse and mistaken opinions, the consecration given in Christian initiation and in the Christian priesthood stood firm and unchangeable. This belief in the stability of status, with belief in the permanence of marriage . . . was one of the roots of Christian civilisation, and gave the Christian a firm hold on immediate immutables and tangible fixities, while Roman civilisation crumbled and the uncertainties and insecurities of life increased. A man's faith, a man's baptism, a man's priest, a man's wife and family, were his for ever, and nothing could take them away. These were a bond of unity, for unity demands stability, between man and man, between generation and generation, and were an essential part of the framework on which Christian civilisation was built. (*Principles of Sacramental Theology*, p. 223)

I have quoted this passage, despite its old-fashioned feel, because it provides a neat summary of Augustine's other contribution to the developing concept of personhood. The belief that we are what we are because God has called us and given us an irrevocable status is just as much part of his legacy as his inward journey to God. It takes us back to an earlier meaning of *persona* as role, but a role this time, not as a victim of cosmic fate, nor as a citizen of an earthly city, but as one graciously chosen by God to have a place in his eternal purposes.

This chapter has concentrated mainly on the theological contribution to the meaning of the word 'person' at the beginning of the Christian era. Many other factors were also at work, among them the growth of individualism in a period of increasing anxiety about the stability of Roman society. The contrast between the high point of Greek drama, when *Antigone* was first performed, and the spectacular brutalities of the amphitheatre during the decline of the Roman Empire, speaks volumes about what had happened to human self-understanding. A late-Roman epitaph sums it up: 'I was; I am not; I do not care.'

Christians, however, did care and carried forward into the future a complex understanding of human personality combining concepts of distinctness, relatedness and substantial reality. Above all, they believed that human life could only be evaluated adequately in its relationship with God. In what follows we shall see how that vision began to disintegrate, and with what consequences.

Persons and individuals

There is a haunting little poem by Elizabeth Jennings in which she describes her feelings in a garden, comparing herself to Eve in the garden of Eden.

When the gardener has gone this garden
Looks wistful and seems waiting an event.
It is so spruce, a metaphor of Eden
And even more so since the gardener went,

Quietly godlike, but, of course, he had
Not made me promise anything, and I
Had no one tempting me to make the bad
Choice. Yet I still felt lost and wonder why.

Even the beech tree from next door which shares
Its shadow with me, seemed a kind of threat.
Everything was too neat and someone cares

In the wrong way. I need not have stood long
Mocked by the smell of a mown lawn, and yet
I did. Sickness for Eden was so strong.

The poem came to mind as I reflected on the rich profusion of theology bequeathed to the Church by Augustine and his predecessors, and the neat – too neat – legacy of Boethius, one of his major interpreters. Some tidying up of the jungle was perhaps inevitable, but there is also a sense of something lost.

In the last chapter I tried to give a flavour of the exciting period of discovery in which new concepts were being created to express new and extraordinary truths. It was a time full of perilous potential, as Eden was, in which fundamental beliefs about God and humanity, and the relation between them, were at stake. But a century later, in the early sixth century, things were very different. Rome had fallen and was ruled by a heretical Goth. East and West were deeply divided. There were new ecclesiastical controversies, not this time focused on the Trinity, but on the Person and Nature of Christ. In what sense could Christ be One Person in Two Natures?

Boethius sought to bring some order and consistency into Christian thinking. He has been described as the 'last of the Romans, and first of the scholastics'. His writings formed a bridge between classical learning and medieval theology. As one of the few Romans in his day who had studied Plato and Aristotle, he aimed to bring a clearer logic to bear on the theological tradition, bedevilled as it still was by a thoroughly confused terminology, and to give it firmer philosophical foundations. The word *persona*, as we have already seen, was a potent source of misunderstanding, being used of individual human beings, the Persons of the Trinity, the Person of God and the Person of Christ, with slightly different meanings in each case.

Like Augustine, Boethius was not keen on the use of the word for the Persons of the Trinity; in fact, for him its introduction was a source of problems rather than a solution to them. He preferred to describe the differentiation within the Trinity in terms of relations, rather than imply the existence of three individual substances which were nevertheless somehow one. Aristotle had, for instance, analysed the master/slave relationship as one in which there is a real distinction, yet complete interdependence. A master can only be a master if there is a slave, and vice versa. Hence the relationship is not just notional, or an aspect of their being, but expresses a fundamental reality. Might the same be true of the Father/Son relationship within the Trinity? Boethius' point was that it is logically possible to speak about differentiations within the being of God, which are just as real as the language of *personae* was intended to be, but which are expressed entirely in relational terms. Freed from its association with the Trinity, the confusing word 'person' could then be given a more precise and limited meaning.

Boethius' attempt to make sense of Christ as having two Natures in one Person led him into further deep waters. There was already a useful distinction between 'nature' and 'person', set out by a monk called Maxentius. Human nature, he had taught, underlies and in some sense precedes human personality. Thus the human embryo may have a fully formed human nature from the start, but develops into a *persona* as it grows in the womb. Nature and personality are therefore related, but different, and it is not impossible to imagine two natures in a single person. Clarifications of this kind, however, had not been enough to heal the divisions which were then racking the Church. Boethius' strategy was to tidy up Augustine by exploring the logical implications of Adam's state before the Fall. If this unfallen state is what is meant by Christ's human nature, and if, as he argued, Adam had been truly able not to sin, then some of the paradox in having both a human and a divine nature begins to be resolved. The two Natures in Christ may perfectly coincide in the one Person, because in his case human nature and the divine intention for human nature are one.

Such rarefied arguments may not have much appeal today. Nevertheless, there is a significant echo of them in the more directly biblical idea that human nature can, at least in an anticipatory sense, bear the image of the divine, a sense which the New Testament writers see as fulfilled in Christ. The same thought is later carried through into the sacramental doctrine that material reality can bear God's image too.

In exploring what that image was, Boethius was led to make his most frequently quoted contribution to philosophy and theology, his definition of 'person' as 'individual substance of a rational nature'. It is a definition which can be used of God as well as of human beings. Medieval theologians had some doubts about the word 'individual' as applied to God, but it seems that it was just acceptable if it carried the meanings of uniqueness and distinctiveness. 'Substance', as we have already seen, had become a key concept in the understanding of *persona*; it is an assertion of real existence. 'Rational nature' was a description of human beings taken straight from Aristotle and is implicit in the Greek concept of an ordered cosmos, capable of being understood by an ordered, i.e. rational, mind. Boethius' Platonism led him to see the archetype of this order in the heavens, just as his Aristotelianism told him that a rational order must have a rational cause. Rationality, in other words, is an attribute both of the human person and of the divine.

Missing from this definition was any acknowledgment that persons have bodies. 'Substance' implicitly included material as well as spiritual substance, but physicality for Boethius seems to have fitted more comfortably within his description of human nature than in his definition of 'person'; hence the definition maintained and extended and, in a sense, institutionalised Augustine's emphasis on inwardness.

Also missing was the idea that persons exist in relation to one another. Of course relationships were recognised as important; Christians could hardly think otherwise, given the link between love of God and love of neighbour. But in Boethius' definition, relationship was not seen as belonging to the essence of personality, as in expositions of the Trinity which described the relationships within it as relationship between Persons in the full sense. The emphasis on individual substance led, rather, in the opposite direction, towards the isolation and independence of the person.

Boethius' tidying up operation was necessary if the Church was to do more than declare what had been revealed, and show that its faith was rationally coherent; for good or ill, he laid the foundations of medieval scholasticism. It was necessary, too, as a means of clarifying what was really at stake in the destructive controversies over subtle and ill-defined points of doctrine. But, as in Elizabeth Jennings' garden, something was also lost. It is possible to care about neatness 'in the wrong way', which in this context may mean missing the point that some concepts are inherently open ended. A word like 'health', for example, has no precise definition because, although it is usually possible to recognise its absence, there is no obvious upper limit to what health itself may entail. The same is true of persons. In a sense everybody knows what persons are. Yet there can be no definition capable of capturing the full reality, not even when used of human beings, still less when used of God.

It is not surprising, therefore, that Boethius' definition, powerful though it was, should eventually reveal some disastrous limitations. To explore them we need to look more closely at the two words 'individual' and 'rational'.

Individual

When Boethius used the word 'individual' he seems to have had in mind two meanings. Literally it means indivisible, or uncuttable, the Greek form of which has given us our word 'atom'. It is that which cannot be divided into parts without destroying its essential nature. Cut a human being in half and the result is not two human beings, but no human being at all. If we consider humanity as a whole, we might describe persons, individual substances, as the smallest units, the atoms of the human world as it were. This is the obvious sense of the phrase, in which we recognise persons as individuals simply by observing their separate existence.

It is a way of thinking which soon runs into difficulties, however. Exactly what is it which cannot be divided? If it is right to think of persons as bodies and souls, then should we think of these as indivisible? There can clearly be bodies without souls – as when we are dead. There can be incomplete bodies – as seriously damaged as the body of Tony Bland. But can there be souls without bodies? If there can, and if, as in Boethius' day, there is a presumption that souls possess a basic unity, then is it to this invisible and indivisible core of personality that the word 'individual' refers, i.e. primarily to some inner spiritual reality? This is the direction in which subsequent thinking was to move. As we shall see later, the notion that a person is an isolated 'inner self' became for many people an unquestioned assumption, and its roots are to be found in this Boethian interpretation of individuality. Meanwhile, we must look at the other meaning which he seems to have had in mind.

'Individual' can also mean singular or distinctive. Each thing is what it is, and not another thing. Each person is distinct from other persons, and one way of symbolising this is by giving each a proper name. To be nameless is rightly regarded as a tragic fate and deliberately to take away somebody's name, as happened in the concentration camps, is to depersonalise them. The substitution of numbers for names in prison says something about those who are temporarily rejected by society. As numbers they become no more than particular instances of the general class of prisoners. All people do, of course, belong to a general class of human beings, and possess some common characteristics which we call human nature, but to be a person is more that this. It is not just to be a member of a class. There is something irreducibly special and individual about each person's existence. It is a meaning of the word which builds on what was said in the previous paragraph about the isolated inner self, by further emphasising each person's uniqueness. It eventually gave rise to the notion of 'the individual' as designating the fundamental reality of what persons are, and hence to individualism as a social and political philosophy.

Thus the net result of Boethius' use of the word was to direct attention away from the concept of persons as existing always in relation to one another, and to give new prominence to their separateness. Obviously he was not responsible for this alone. Other factors, notably social and economic changes, and much later theological revolutions – notably Protestantism – were to give an enormous impetus in the same direction. But the enduring popularity of Boethius' definition is a sign that it represented the way people were actually beginning to think about themselves, a way in marked contrast to what had gone before.

As we saw in the last chapter, the early communities described in the Old Testament were of a kind which allowed little sense of individuality. The idea of God 'visiting the iniquity of the fathers upon the children unto the third and fourth generation of them that hate me; and showing mercy unto thousands of them that love me, and keep my commandments' (Exod. 20:5), was no idle threat. The punishment of whole families, and even whole cities or nations, for the sins of one of their members – as in the story of the stoning of Achan and his whole family for disobeying the command not to loot Jericho after its capture by Joshua (Josh. 7) – was regarded as a proper corollary of group solidarity. The early prophets interpreted the sufferings of the whole nation in terms of the intimate relationship between sinful rulers and their people. This was not the whole story. The Psalms, with their emphasis on personal piety and their pleas about individual reward and punishment, are a warning against interpretations too heavily biased in the direction of community consciousness. There was also a distinct shift in prophetic emphasis at the time when Israel went into exile, losing the sense of being a settled community. The very fact of being in an alien culture forced a change of ideas, and the notion of personal accountability began to take firmer root. Both Jeremiah and Ezekiel were concerned that the Jews in exile should not put the blame for all their troubles on other people, or previous generations, or an anonymous 'them'. In a famous passage in Ezekiel (18:2–4) the prophet in exile deliberately reverses the warning in the Ten Commandments:

What mean ye that ye use this proverb concerning
the land of Israel, saying, The fathers have eaten
sour grapes, and the children's teeth are set on
edge? As I live, saith the Lord God, ye shall not
have occasion any more to use this proverb in
Israel. Behold, all souls are mine; as the soul of
the father, so also the soul of the son is mine: the
soul that sinneth it shall die.

Interdependent

Personal accountability is one thing, though, and
individualism is another. In the ancient world
accountability was always understood within the
context of a community. Aristotle, for instance, in
exploring what it means to be a good man, saw
individual goodness as inseparable from active participation as a citizen in the life of a good city. Extract
men from their context as members of a political
community, and they lose some of their essential
attributes. Incidentally, my use of the word 'man' in
this context is not accidental; in classical Greece
women and slaves were not part of the political
community, but had their place in the household which
operated by a kind of despotism in which individuals
counted for little. The household, according to Hannah
Arendt, was the realm of necessity, providing the basic
supports for life; the city was a man's world, the realm
of freedom. Responsible individuality, therefore, had
its limits.

St Paul's vision of the body of Christ is another

famous example of the kind of interdependence which required its members to be personally accountable – in fact he exhorts each one of them, like the organs of a body, to play their allotted part, but always for the good of the whole, not as separate individuals. There is a striking passage in Karl Barth's *Church Dogmatics* where he says that the starting point for any thinking about what he calls 'the basic form of humanity' must be the humanity of the man Jesus; and it is a starting point which excludes the possibility of seeing people in isolation.

> If we do not realize and take into account from the very outset ... the fact that [man] has a neighbour, we do not see him at all ... The fact that the Good Shepherd has acted on behalf of his lost sheep shows that he does not give it up for lost but still numbers it with his flock and deals with it as his own and not an alien possession. This is what makes the idea of a man without his fellows, in any form, quite intolerable (III, 2, p. 227).

He then drives the point home with a long exposition about Nietzsche as the most perceptive and dangerous enemy of Christian morality.

> The new thing in Nietzsche was the man of 'azure isolation', six thousand feet above time and man; the man to whom a fellow-creature drinking at the same well is quite dreadful and insufferable; the man who is utterly inaccessible to others,

having no friends and despising women; the man
who is at home only with the eagles and strong
winds ... (III, 2, p. 240).

In other words, this is the apotheosis of individualism,
Nietzsche's superman.

These are powerful statements which need to be set
alongside what is said in the Gospels about the
Heavenly Father's care for individuals, even to the
counting of the hairs on one's head. Persons *are*
individuals in the sense of being unique realities –
perhaps a better expression than 'individual substance'.
This uniqueness always exists within the context of
other unique realities, however, and cannot be itself
without them. This is the truth which Nietzsche hated,
and which individualistic philosophies of self-
realisation and self-fulfilment tend to dismiss.

Theologians, particularly in the Orthodox tradition,
have another way of making the point – by seeing the
word 'individual' as a description of our common lot
as fallen human beings. What we have in common as
part of our ordinary human nature, a nature disfigured
by sin, is the fact that we are units in competition with
one another. Starting from this sense of separation, we
set our individual wills over against each other. But
'persons', as understood theologically, should be just
the opposite; the unique reality of a person is that of
being in the image of God, and it as those who
participate together in that image that we find our true
selves. As in all Orthodox theology, the basis of self-
understanding lies in the doctrine of the Trinity, in the
mutual self-giving of the Persons of the Trinity, and in

the love that unites them. To be made in this image and to share in this mutuality of love makes the idea of being no more than an individual ego, or worse, a self-created man, seem if not blasphemous, at least faintly ludicrous.

Rational

None of what has just been said is intended to deny that persons are individuals. It is the weight given to the word 'individual', and the implications drawn from it, which can tip the balance towards ego-centricity. The danger can be compounded by mistaken interpretations of the other term in Boethius' definition, which raises some equally serious problems.

If a person is an 'individual substance of a rational nature', it would seem that the key attribute of personhood is reason. The fact is that many people are not reasonable, and that Freud and his followers have thrown the gravest doubts on whether any of us are, are not in themselves grounds for criticising the definition. To have a rational nature implies that we can in certain circumstances reason soundly, not that we always do.

The belief that what distinguishes human beings from all other species can be located in a special faculty called 'Reason' is built into the fabric of Western thought. Boethius accepted the classic distinction between rational and irrational beings, and until comparatively recent times it would not have occurred to most philosophers or theologians to question it. Philosophers in particular tended to live in cities where they had little contact with 'brute beasts', and theologians relied on the first chapter of Genesis where the contrast between man and the rest of creation could not have been drawn more sharply.

What *is* reason? It is one of those words in constant use and widely understood, but extremely difficult to define. It is easier to point to examples of good reasoning, as when I listen to the weather forecast and decide to take an umbrella, than to say precisely what it is. Definition is made harder by the fact that it is used with a variety of contraries, reason and unreason, for instance, or reason and faith, reason and emotion, reason and intelligence, with the word 'reason' having different nuances in each context.

If we return for a moment to the case of Tony Bland and ask what reason tells us should have been done, the answer will depend on the contrast being drawn. An unreasonable response on the part of his parents might have been to look for revenge – to sue the hospital, or the police, or the football club – as an alternative to calm acceptance of the situation, to being 'reasonable' in fact. Irrational behaviour might have a slightly different nuance. It is probably irrational to fill a hospital room with football memorabilia. Cold calculation suggests that it is useless, but to be so rational as to allow no place for sentiment is, in another sense, unreasonable. There is such a thing as reasonable emotion, just as there are times when emotion – say, an exaggerated sense of guilt and refusal to forgive oneself – has to yield to reason. What seems to have sustained Tony Bland's parents during their long, three-year vigil was a kind of faith, a willingness to hope against hope, not to give up despite the growing weight of objective evidence that recovery was not possible. Was it a reasonable faith? In their case it was sadly disappointed. But there have been subsequent cases in which the diagnosis of PVS has proved wrong, and the persistence of those who have loved, and hoped, and searched for tiny signs of improvement has been vindicated. There are times when the question of whether or not a faith is reasonable can only be answered by experience.

A tragic situation like that of Tony Bland evokes a whole gamut of responses. My aim in spelling out a few of them has simply been to illustrate different forms which the exercise of reason can take. In fact, reason is not a 'thing' which always operates in the same way, and which human beings either do or do not possess. It is more a description of a certain type of reflective behaviour, dependent on innate mental capacities, which can be exercised in different contexts and to greater or lesser degrees. Intellect, which is clearly one aspect of it, is the ability to perceive, to discriminate, to form mental concepts, and in that sense to understand. It is a capacity human beings share, to varying extents, with some other animals, and there is nothing anomalous, for instance, in ascribing intelligence to a sheepdog. Sheepdogs could not do their work without perceiving, discriminating, understanding, and in some measure thinking. Ancient philosophers might have thought differently about animal intelligence if they had seen such a dog in action; still more so if they had observed chimpanzees.

Human powers of reasoning require a minimum level of intelligence, but what seems to be special about us, though even this may not be entirely unique, is our capacity for self-awareness and abstraction. These will be major topics in Chapters 7 and 8, but the essential point to be made at this stage is that reasoning is about thinking at one or more removes from immediate or instinctive reaction. An intelligent sheepdog reacts to a command, but the man blowing the whistle is thinking about the next move, anticipating what the sheep might do, and keeping his eye on his watch. He is performing a complex, planned operation, and knows that he is.

One of the legacies of Greek thought was the tendency to regard mathematics and logic as the most typical expressions of reason, with the result that reasoning came to be regarded as a form of calculating. It is an idea which still grips many people's imagination and gives plausibility to the belief that artificial intelligence as versatile as that of humans will one day be possible. But all that was a long way in the future when Boethius made his definition. Simple rules of logic, like the rule that forbids contradictions, were much nearer the heart of the matter and have remained so. If reason allows contradictions, then anything can be deduced from anything, and systematic thinking becomes impossible. Lewis Carroll, who wrote a major textbook on logic, used to have fun in twisting it slightly, often with the aid of puns, to produce absurd results. When Humpty Dumpty advised Alice to stop growing, she replied indignantly, 'One can't help growing older.' '*One* can't, perhaps,' said Humpty Dumpty, 'but *two* can. With proper assistance you might have left off at seven.' Alice wisely changed the subject.

So powerful is the concept of logical reasoning that strenuous attempts were made at the turn of this century to prove that mathematics itself could be deduced entirely from logic, and that language was only meaningful in so far as it could be reduced to a series of strictly logical terms. Neither attempt was successful, and good reasons were discovered why they could not be. Indeed, the Greeks had known, more than two centuries earlier, that although calculation is an important part of reasoning, it cannot be the whole of it. There also has to be insight, a grasp of first principles, an intuitive apprehension of what is good and right, without which the business of deductive reasoning cannot get started.

In some ways this is analogous to faith. St Anselm's famous saying, 'Believe in order that you may understand,' is making the same point. But neither Socrates nor Anselm was advocating a leap of faith as an alternative to reason. Having started with what we believe to be right and good, there has to follow a prolonged process of testing. It is this testing, largely through argument, and amendment of the initial assumptions where necessary, which gradually builds up a tradition of ideas and premises which can form the basis for deductive reasoning. This is why Greek philosophy was generally written in the form of dialogues, in which various characters raised all the objections they could think of against whatever idea was being proposed. The ideas which survived this battery of criticism could then be regarded as the best approximation to truth available at that stage in the argument.

Reason, on this understanding, could thus be located within a long and well-tested tradition of thinking, always open to dispute and correction, and constantly having to prove itself by its ability to make sense of actual experience. In so far as it could show how to make better sense of the insights of one of its rivals, then this could be counted as further evidence of its validity.

This method of discerning truth through argument, which owes its origin to Socrates, has strong resemblances to what we now know as the scientific method. The difference is that it was essentially based on ideas, rather than on empirical evidence. It has proved its worth over the centuries, particularly in moral philosophy, but was in many people's eyes discredited by being taken to extreme lengths in medieval scholasticism. Some of the much debated philosophical and theological ideas during that period were very remote from ordinary experience. The example always quoted, with liberal doses of ridicule, is the dispute over how many angels can dance on the head of a pin. In fact it may not have been so silly as it is made out to be. How else would a medieval theologian philosophise about the nature of space?

Despite excesses, the method of continuing debate and criticism within a well-tested tradition still seems the only way of reasoning about such fundamental questions as, for example, what counts as an explanation. Questions like these fall outside science, because they are prior to it. Our powers of reasoning are shaped by our basic values, commitments, assumptions and insights, which like everything else have to be put to the test by experience – including the experience of other people. We cannot claim to be reasonable if we have no contact with some such process.

The implications of this for Boethius' definition are profound. Our rational nature is not simply given. We may have innate capacities, but neither logic nor insight can come to fruition outside a continuing historical process which involves a whole community of people. We talk nowadays about the scientific community in which a certain kind of rationality is constantly debated, tested and refined. Boethius and his medieval successors would have understood this. They belonged within a tradition whose very method made the community context obvious. But it was eventually to change. Increasing emphasis on the individual, and the tendency to think of reason as an innate faculty possessed by each such individual, eroded the concept of reasoning as a communal process within a tested tradition, and was to have disastrous consequences in the future.

However neat a garden may be, it never stays that way for long, and sometimes the things which grow strongest are not what one might have wished.

5

The vanishing person

When Jacques Delors was President of the European Commission, he used to like calling together groups of what he was pleased to call 'intellectuals' to guide the Commission in policy-making. I was lucky enough to attend two of these gatherings – on Science, Conscience and Society – which ranged widely over such issues as the philosophy of science, science and ethics, science policy in Europe, and the role of the Commission itself. They were enjoyable occasions, but what intrigued me most were the assumptions which undergirded the whole exercise. Delors was in effect asking us to identify the fundamental principles on which science policy should be based. If the Commission was to do its work, he believed, it needed a clear and well-articulated philosophy to help it define its aims, and it was automatically assumed that the right people to produce this were a miscellaneous bunch of intellectuals.

The whole exercise seemed to me very French. The French education system still gives great weight to philosophy. It is the job of the thinker to produce clear and distinct ideas. Policy decisions follow from these through a process of logical reasoning, and the bureaucratic orderliness of French society – and to a lesser extent of the European Commission – is one of the consequences. Napoleon also casts his shadow; it was he who tried to impose logic on social organisation, even to the point of devising a mathematically logical calendar.

The trouble is that science policy does not, and cannot, work like this. The most creative scientists thrash around, follow hunches, come to dead ends, have lucky breaks, and in general behave like most other human beings. Though they value order and logic when thinking about the inner coherence and verification of scientific hypotheses, they do not feel constrained by them in the process of discovery. Discovery, in fact, can be a chaotic business, and the same might be said of our rather expensive international gatherings. I doubt whether the Commission got much good advice.

I tell this story because what I have described as 'very French' had its origins in the key figure in French philosophy, who for centuries dominated his country's education, and is still regarded as the founding father of modern Western European philosophy. In trying to understand the different ways in which we have come to think of ourselves as persons, it is impossible to avoid René Descartes (1596–1650).

Much happened in the 1,100 years between Boethius and Descartes, but it is not hard to trace how the concepts of individuality and rationality, discussed in the last chapter, contained within them the seeds of much later, and very different, ideas. Thus in leaping from Boethius to Descartes, from the sixth to the seventeenth century, my aim is simply to point out connections, not to attempt the enormous task of recounting history.

One of the ancient tests of rationality, as we have seen, was to subject all claims to truth to every possible kind of criticism. Whatever survived the criticism was held to be the closest approximation to truth then available. Hence the traditional form of philosophy was the dialogue, in which ideas were put forward, doubts expressed and arguments refuted. Doubting was a necessary and integral part of learning, and criticism was seen as the lifeblood of knowledge.

Suppose, however, one decides to doubt absolutely everything. Is there any point at which the doubting has to stop? Is there anything which can be known with certainty and clarity? This was the question Descartes asked himself on a momentous day in 1619. He was a mathematician, and was convinced that the methods of mathematics should be applied to all other studies, because it alone could provide clear, logical and guaranteed reasoning. He determined 'never to accept anything for true which I did not clearly know to be such ... to divide difficulties under examination into as many parts as possible ... to conduct my thoughts in such order that, by commencing with objects the simplest and easiest to know, I might ascend by little and little ... to the knowledge of the more complex.' Here in a nutshell was the essence of scientific method, and it is no coincidence that Descartes was writing at a time when modern science was being born, nor that he became the philosopher who provided its rationale.

Where to begin? The only thing Descartes could not doubt was the fact that he himself was thinking – the famous statement 'I think, therefore I am.' It was a starting point which took as read, and exaggerated, some of the themes we have already seen emerging in Boethius. The concept of the rational individual was subtly transformed into that of the solitary thinker with a mind wholly distinct from, and more directly known than, the body. Rationality itself was limited to what could be clearly and distinctly expressed, preferably in the language of mathematics.

For Augustine the inner life had been his way to the knowledge of God. For Descartes it was the way to the only certainty available – his own most immediate experience. This concentration on the inner self was not intended to exclude God. In fact, Descartes believed God was necessary to his philosophy, by providing the assurance that there was an orderly and comprehensible reality outside himself. His contemporary Blaise Pascal (1623–62), also a mathematician, saw the weakness in this argument and realised that God so conceived was marginal, and would eventually be removed as redundant. He wrote, 'I cannot forgive Descartes. In all his philosophy he would have been quite willing to dispense with God. But he had to make Him give a fillip to set the world in motion; beyond this, he has no further need of God.' Pascal realised that a philosophy which begins with the inner self, and is tied to mathematical logic, must in the end exclude morality, judgment and all that is most characteristically human. When God is made redundant, humanity quickly follows.

It was centuries before the full implications of Descartes' philosophy could be seen. But long before its disastrous consequences had become apparent, it had set the agenda for a new understanding of what it is to be a person. In what follows I shall look first at the rigid distinction drawn by Descartes between mind and matter; then at the impetus he gave to a particular view of reason; and finally at the consequences of starting with the solitary thinker.

Mind and matter

Dualism is the name given to the belief that mind and matter are completely distinct realities. It has obvious attractions in that it seems to accord with common sense. There is a different quality to the direct and private access we have to our own minds, and our knowledge of the public world which we perceive through our senses and interpret with our minds. What is 'out there' we call matter, and what is 'in here' we call mind, and Descartes seemed entirely plausible in claiming that the one cannot be reduced to the other. A similar dualism also seems to be implied by traditional language about souls and bodies. Like mind and matter, these are frequently described as if they were two distinct entities, one of them spiritual and the other material, which together make up the human person. Of the two, the soul has usually been regarded by religious believers as the more important because, being immaterial and eternal, it can provide a basis for believing in life after death.

Such claims have relevance to the case of Tony Bland. If dualism is true, then there must have been some point in time when his soul left his body and he could be pronounced dead, no matter how much residual life his body still seemed to contain. As we saw in Chapter 2, however, there were actually great difficulties in deciding whether there was any such moment, and whether it was meaningful to try to discern it. If, as was suggested, death may be a process rather than an event, does it still make any sense to define it in terms of the departure of the soul? This is only a particular instance of the general difficulty encountered by dualism as it seeks to relate mind and matter, body and soul, in a way which does not give rise to insoluble problems. The most difficult of these problems is how, if they are entirely distinct, is it possible for them to interact? Descartes postulated a particular part of the brain – the pineal gland, which then had no known function – as the place where the interaction takes place. This was quickly seen to be a nonsense, and in any case tells us nothing about what such interaction would have to entail. It is an issue which has haunted dualism ever since, and I look at it again in more detail in Chapter 7 when considering the nature of consciousness.

Meanwhile, it is important to note that neither Greek ideas about body and soul, nor the subsequent theology based on them, ran into the same problems as the kind of dualism proposed by Descartes. Nor, though this was not well recognised at the time, did

Hebraic ideas about the psychosomatic unity of human beings fit into the dualistic pattern. In Aristotle's philosophy and its medieval interpretations the soul was not treated as a separate entity distinct from the body, but was identified as the 'form' of the body, that which gave it its particular characteristics as a living human organism. The soul is, as it were, the inner reality, of which the body is the outward expression. On this understanding the question of interaction does not arise, since soul and body are essentially one. We might compare soul and body, for example, to the meaning and the actual written words of a book. The meaning cannot be separated from the words in which the book is written, yet they are not the same. The meaning is *in* the words, but is not identical to them. In fact, if the book is translated into another language, virtually the same meaning can be conveyed in quite different words, and the very possibility of translation depends on the assumption that words and meanings are in principle separable, even though the one cannot exist without the other. In some such way one might envisage a soul being translated into another body, and there has been much speculation among philosophers about the implications of this for personal identity. Christian theologians have on the whole welcomed the concept of translatability, in that it harmonises with the belief that life after death requires a resurrection body, not just the continuance of a disembodied soul.

To hold to Christian beliefs about the soul, in other words, need not entail the kind of dualism advocated by Descartes. As we shall see later, there are less drastic methods of demonstrating how consciousness, and all that is included under the headings of self, soul and spirit, cannot be explained, or explained away, merely in terms of physical descriptions.

The world as machine

Descartes, by his choice of the one reality he could not doubt, highlighted the enormous philosophical significance of self-awareness. The word 'I' is unique, and each of us enjoys a unique, first-person perspective on the whole of our experience. This much is obvious. Unfortunately, though, Descartes expressed this uniqueness in a way which entailed a complete separation between the thinking, experiencing person, and the world about which they were thinking. The world, as one half of this duality, came to be regarded as a mere thing, a machine, an object for mathematical analysis. This was a shift in perspective which had a liberating effect on science, set new standards of precision, and delivered scientific thinking from the comforting belief that understanding could be had on vaguer terms. It implied that the natural world was in principle capable of being explained by methods and categories which owed nothing to theology, morality or purpose. Nature could thus be investigated with an open mind, and there was no need to be entangled in the kind of religious issues which had bedevilled Galileo and nearly brought him to the stake.

The separation into different spheres of study, and eventually into different academic disciplines, was to be a vital factor in the growth of modern knowledge, and had already been anticipated by Descartes in his proposal to investigate complex matters by breaking them down into simpler parts. The study of the function of blood, for example, could make no real progress until the simple mechanics of blood circulation could first be examined separately from all the religious and emotional overtones associated with blood and heart – overtones which began to resonate again when the first heart transplant was performed, centuries after the discovery that the heart's role is no more than that of a simple pump. In the same way the study of the solar system had first to be detached from any prior beliefs about the way God must have made it, before astronomers were free to concentrate on the accumulation of data and the invention of techniques of mathematical analysis powerful enough to make sense of such an enormous quantity of figures. I remember my own first science lesson, when we were made to learn the text, 'Science is measurement.'

The belief that the world could be understood as a machine gave scientists a goal and a method, and was enormously productive. But there was a price to pay. It is a price which has become more and more obvious in the twentieth century, as we see the consequences for the environment of detaching human, moral and religious concerns from the power, unleashed by scientific discovery, to exploit nature and mould it to our desires. Many people by now feel alienated from a view of the world which seems to have no place for truly human values. There is widespread revulsion, too, at one of the other results of Descartes' division of reality into a rational thinking part and a purely mechanical part. Animals, in contrast to human beings, fell on the wrong side of the line. They were described as mere machines, lacking reason and self-awareness. Their cries of pain were the squeaks in the machine; their writhings were no more than unconscious reflexes. It was a philosophy which fitted well with the instincts of the time to treat so-called soulless beasts as created simply for human use and pleasure. But even then there were perceptive critics who saw that if this were done to animals, it would not be long before it were done to human beings. As more and more specifically human experience was pigeonholed and 'explained' in mechanical terms, the non-mechanical half of Descartes' world, the isolated thinking self, began to seem more and more insubstantial. The person was in danger of vanishing – like Lewis Carroll's Cheshire Cat.

The rational mind

The citadel of personhood was located by Descartes in the ability to think, and it is to this part of his legacy, and his emphasis on a particular concept of rationality, that we must now turn. He was content with nothing less than 'clear and distinct ideas', and he was convinced that the best model for reasoning with such ideas was provided by mathematics. In this, as in his dualism, he set the scene for modern science. The natural sciences have achieved their successes by developing clearly defined concepts, such as mass, energy, velocity and voltage, which can be quantified and whose behaviour can thus be studied mathematically. The concepts are not obvious, and in the pioneering phase of a science the most crucial advances usually lie in the invention of concepts which are sufficiently clear and distinct to be treated in this way.

By contrast, the so-called 'soft sciences', such as sociology and psychology, which belong as it were to the second wave of scientific advance, have had great difficulty in developing such clearly defined and generally agreed concepts, and hence lack the precision to be found in physics or chemistry. Soft sciences are a reminder that the closer we come to actual human life, the less attainable are the standards laid down by Descartes, and the less appropriate is mathematics as a tool for handling imprecise ideas. Such considerations do not, of course, deter some physicists in their search for a 'theory of everything', by which they mean a mathematical formula uniting all the fundamental theories of physics; but it would seem that 'everything' in their book does not include human beings.

The mathematical ambitions expressed by Descartes did not in the first instance lead in the direction of this kind of absurdity. He had already excluded the human mind from the world of nature to which the new scientists were going to devote their attention. This still left the question of what the mind actually does. If its distinguishing characteristic is rationality, how is this to be understood? As we have seen, there was a long tradition which had identified reason with logic

and calculation. In the first flush of excitement at the
new philosophy, ancient Greek logic was derided as
nothing more than playing around with abstractions,
and the idea of attaining insight into truth by sustained
argument seemed hopelessly airy-fairy in comparison
with exact observation and mathematical analysis. In
time, however, the general preoccupation with mathematical explanation was to lead to a subtle change of
emphasis in perceptions of the mind itself. By the mid-
nineteenth century the two Greek systems of logic,
devised respectively by Aristotle and the Stoics, were
being set out in a quasi-mathematical notation, which
could then be used for making logical calculations,
just as in mathematics. In other words, the idea that
logical thinking is essentially a form of calculation was
no longer a speculation, but was being given practical
application. From there it was only a small step to
mechanising the operation, and the result is staring
me in the face as I type these words on a computer,
which seems for most of the time to behave with
modest intelligence, yet is in fact no more than a
calculating machine operating according to logical
rules, previously fed into it by employees of the
ubiquitous Mr Gates.

The point of recounting this absurdly potted history
has simply been to make the connection between the
concept of reason assumed by Descartes, and the
eventual assimilation of thinking – the very capacity
he specified as distinctive of the mind – into the
mechanical world with which he had contrasted it.
The wheel has come full circle. If thinking is no more
than calculation, and if calculation can be done by

machines, then what is there to distinguish human beings from very clever machines? Once again we are aware of the vanishing person.

What has gone wrong? There were from the start clear signs that all was not well with the concept of rationality which has sustained this rake's progress. I have already referred to the soft sciences, particularly concerned with human life, which cannot be fitted into the mathematical straitjackets those working in the harder sciences would like to devise for them.

In Chapter 8 I shall look more closely at the limitations of a logic tied too closely to the mathematical model. Meanwhile, it is worth noting that when Descartes was writing, Pascal already saw the dangers. He began his famous *Pensées* by drawing a contrast between 'the mathematical and the intuitive mind'. Mathematicians reason correctly from clear principles, he wrote, but they often do not see what is obvious to those who perceive things directly and as a whole. 'Mathematicians wish to treat matters of intuition mathematically, and make themselves ridiculous, wishing to begin with definitions and then with axioms, which is not the way to proceed in this kind of reasoning. Not that the mind does not do so, but it does it tacitly, naturally, and without technical rules . . .' Pascal did not deny that thought is the distinctive characteristic of human beings. 'Man is but a reed, the most feeble thing in nature; but he is a thinking reed . . . all our dignity consists, then, in thought. By it we must elevate ourselves, and not by space and time which we cannot fill. Let us endeavour, then, to think well; this is the principle of morality.'

What he wanted to do, though, was to call attention to other modes of thinking, those not included under the heading of calculation, and which concerned him, not so much as a mathematician – indeed one of the best mathematicians of his age – but as a human being. His most frequently quoted words are: 'The heart has its reasons, which reason does not know,' to which he added the question, 'Is it by reason that you love yourself?'

If Pascal were writing today, he would probably not have used the word 'intuition' which has come to have a rather more individualistic and subjective feel than I believe he intended. Words such as insight, judgment and perceptiveness seem closer to his meaning, but one of the clearest accounts of these other dimensions in rational thinking is to be found in the writings of the twentieth-century philosopher of science, Michael Polanyi. He spoke of tacit or inarticulate knowledge, the things of which we are aware, and the skills we exercise, without being able to say precisely what they are, or how they are done. Theologians, in particular, are only too well aware of the limitations of language and logic. In the last resort theology is an attempt to express the inexpressible. As the Russian philosopher, Nicolas Berdyaev, put it, 'We come to God not because rational thought demands his existence, but because the world is bounded by a mystery in which rational thought ends.'

Postmodernism's critique of the limits of language can lead in the same direction. The more language has been scientifically analysed, the more it has become apparent that it cannot put into unequivocal words all that we know or can experience. The limitations are even more obvious in mathematics. Even quite ordinary activities can defy complete and rigorous analysis. Painting a picture by numbers requires some elementary skills like applying paint cleanly and evenly. But these fall far short of the real skills in painting, which are degraded as soon as they are turned into some kind of formula. How many cyclists can say precisely how they manage to stay upright? How many would learn any quicker, or learn at all, if they were taught by being introduced to the laws of dynamic equilibrium? Rational thought and behaviour include logic, and should rightly strive for precision, but they are not confined to logic, and that is why too narrow a definition of rationality can be so impoverishing.

The isolated self

I turn finally in this chapter to the third element in the legacy of Descartes, his choice of a starting point. 'I think, therefore I am.' At the centre of the universe of knowledge sits the solitary thinker. Everything known is either perceived directly as an object of thought, or is built up from what later generations of philosophers were to call 'sense data', tiny bits of information flowing into the brain through our sensory nerves. The fundamental truth about us, according to this picture, is that we are isolated individual centres of consciousness. The inner world is a kind of observation post, a seeing eye, the point at which all the lines of sight converge.

This is not the only way of seeing the world. I recall once on a visit to Moscow being given a lesson on icons, which included an explanation of why many traditional icon painters appear at first sight to have had a very poor understanding of perspective. The buildings depicted in some icons look childishly perverse, not only architecturally unsound, but with their dimensions seeming to grow larger as they recede into the picture. They are in stark contrast to the beautifully drawn and serene-looking saints who occupy the foreground. Exactly so, explained my guide. The figures represent the beauty of holiness in the midst of a crazy and disordered world which is likely to collapse at any moment. The distortions in the world of objects are deliberate, and it is drawn in reverse perspective, to make the point that the viewer is not the centre of it. The true centre of the world lies elsewhere – in God – and we find him, not by drawing all the lines of sight towards ourselves, but by acknowledging the infinitude of what lies outside us. We are part of his vision, not he of ours.

It is a lesson more easily learnt, perhaps, by those who paint holy pictures in a spirit of prayer than in a society which in the sixteenth and seventeenth centuries was rapidly discovering the supreme significance of the individual. All kinds of forces were at work, social, economic and religious, in helping to establish this new awareness of human persons as solitary centres of consciousness. Philosophers such as Descartes provided the ideas and the language for it, but its roots were nourished elsewhere. This is why revolutions in self-understanding cannot be reversed simply by pointing out philosophical mistakes. They come to be embedded in a complete way of life.

The Renaissance had begun the process of putting human beings in the centre of the world which, like the world of the icon painters, had previously been centred on God. Medieval society had depended on an all-embracing system of obligations and responsibilities, sustained by a hierarchical structure, of which God was the apex. It provided security, but very little freedom. Most people felt themselves to be powerless in the ordering of their own lives, a fact which no doubt strengthened the attraction of religion through its reminder that life is more than servitude – if only beyond the grave. As people's horizons were gradually expanded during the Renaissance, and as the medieval synthesis began to break down, what eventually emerged was the polar opposite of the previous sense of powerlessness – what we now know as autonomous individuality. It was a concept at first still deeply imbued with religion – the individual responsible before God – but contained within it were the seeds of atheism. Berdyaev, again, makes the point sharply:

Renaissance humanism affirmed the autonomy of man, and his freedom in the spheres of cultural creation, science and art. Herein lay its truth, for it was essential that the creative force of humanity should surmount the obstacles and prohibitions that mediaeval Christianity put in its way. Unfortunately, however, the Renaissance also began to assert man's self-sufficiency, and to make a rift between him and the eternal truths of

Christianity . . . Here we have the fountain-head
of the tragedy of modern history . . . God became
the enemy of man, and man the enemy of God.
(Quoted in Norman Davies, *Europe*, p. 479)

Other minds

As the autonomous individual gradually evolved into
Descartes' isolated self, some of the puzzles and
contradictions in this way of thinking began to make
themselves felt. One of the most famous of these is the
problem of 'other minds'. The individual mind had
come to be seen as doubly isolated. There was first an
isolation *between* minds. According to John Locke, one
of the founding fathers of Enlightenment thinking, each
of us builds up our knowledge of the world on the
basis of purely individual perceptions. It was irrational
to suppose that the mind contained what he called
'innate ideas' – as if babies, for example, could have
an innate idea of God. The mind must therefore start
as a blank sheet on which individual experience writes
the text. But this entails a second kind of isolation, an
isolation *from* the raw material of perception. The
world is thought of as an objective reality from which
persons in their inmost being are somehow disengaged.
It is the image of the seeing eye again, which stands
outside what it sees.

What is this seeing eye, this focus of consciousness?
If all knowledge truly starts with a blank sheet, there
are disturbing questions to be asked about whether
there is anything at all at the focal point where the

lines of sight intersect. Am 'I' just the sum of my knowledge and experience? In modern times, rational detachment, the isolation of individuals as separate centres of experience, and the concentration on objective experience as the only reliable clue to the nature of reality, have led many people by a fairly straight route to discount all that seems to them merely personal or inward – or 'mystical', as some like to describe it. To be a person, according to this view, means no more than to possess an information-processing brain.

All of this gives some urgency to the question of whether other minds exist. With Descartes, we may declare that our own minds exist, or at least that we are directly aware of some kind of inner self which is capable of thinking, but how do we know that anybody else has the same experience? We have no direct insight into the inner reality of another person, nor into how the world appears to them. So how can we know that they have minds like ours?

There are tortuous arguments which seek to prove that we can know other people's minds by analogy with our own experience. We can observe them, it is argued, and deduce what they must be thinking and feeling, by comparing their behaviour with our own. Clearly there is some truth in this argument. We do in fact interpret other people's behaviour in the light of our own feelings, and one of the most important social skills is to be able to use such insights to see beyond the behaviour to what must be going on inside. While such skills might help us to empathise, and so to understand *what* people are thinking, however, it is difficult to see how an argument from analogy can help us decide the more basic question as to *whether* they are thinking, because such argument assumes that we have some direct insight into what the analogy refers to.

Admittedly, outside the realm of academic philosophy, it is only in extreme circumstances that questions of this kind become pressing; but we have already met them in the case of Tony Bland. Did he in any sense still have a mind capable of feeling, even though such feelings could find no expression? If he did, how could one ever know? Or how could one know whether some advanced form of artificial intelligence might have an inner life and consciousness, and thus might merit the same respect and protection as a person? Or how could one see into the mind of a being from another planet, given the very low probability of aliens being able to speak our language?

The fact that we do not ask such questions about our ordinary acquaintances is evidence that, for the most part, we simply assume that other people have minds like our own. Our awareness of them feels much more like instinct than logic, and our puzzlement in face of the extreme cases is a symptom of practical doubt about the circumstances, not philosophic doubt about whether other minds exist. Indeed, the artificiality of the philosophical problem lies in the fact that it starts from the wrong place, from the philosopher sitting in his study, contemplating his own sensations, and deciding what he can or cannot know.

In reality nobody starts from there. All of us, even philosophers, start as babies, and we explore our world by interacting with it, and especially by interacting with other people. The isolated individual is an abstraction. We may *make* ourselves isolated, but none of us can *start* isolated, because our humanity is shaped by our relationships with each other. One of the key instruments through which such interactive relationships begin and grow is language, and without it the mind can scarcely develop. The fact that most young children learn to speak almost without trying is evidence that the capacity for it is innate, and that Locke was wrong, therefore, in supposing that the mind starts as a blank sheet. The contents of language have to be learnt from others in the process of exploring and shaping experience. Children so unfortunate as to be without language, either through lack of human contact, or on account of some major disability, suffer terrible mental deprivation. As some of those who have subsequently learnt a language have reported, they had no means of making sense of what they were experiencing. Our mental abilities, in short, are formed by increasingly significant communication between adults and children, and this can only happen if their minds are by and large sharing the same meanings and communicating about the same realities. Children do not deduce that other minds exist; their own minds are formed by those other minds.

It is this sharing and communicating which makes possible our capacity for thought. Whether our thought processes are primarily visual or verbal, both kinds depend ultimately on language. It is through language that we are initiated into a way of thinking about the world, ourselves and other people. Language provides patterns of meaning without which rational thought could have no starting point. It is not the only means of communication, however. In the earliest years of infancy communication is through touch, signs, faces, smiles, and the awareness of another's presence. The process can be described in terms of infants growing into persons through being loved, and this is mutual. If infants could not evoke love as well as receive it, it is hard to see why anybody would persist with them at three o'clock in the morning. In fact, we are back with Austin Farrer's image of human and divine kingship in process of mutual formation. Persons form each other. Parents form their children, and if they are wise they allow themselves to be shaped by their children in return. Thus the philosopher wondering whether other minds exist cuts a rather absurd figure, because knowing other minds is a necessary part of becoming and being ourselves. He can only doubt their reality by ignoring the very factors which have enabled and developed his own capacity to think.

I shall return in Chapter 8 to the question of how much innate capacity is needed for this process of communication to get to work. John Macmurray, who wrote persuasively about the mutual formation of persons, claimed that the only instinctive impulse in the newborn infant is the impulse to communicate – frequently by yelling – and went on to describe this as the essential difference between animals and humans – in whom everything else has to be learnt. I am not sure one need, or can, go as far as that. What is certain, however, is that without communication the distinctive characteristics of human beings could not have come into existence.

Macmurray went on to make the further point that without such interpersonal communication, the Enlightenment programme of depersonalising the external world in order to study it objectively would have been impossible. As individuals we have to make judgments about what we believe is, or is not, true, but we cannot do this in isolation. If we are to identify and study some common external reality, we are also heavily dependent on the judgments of others. We can only claim a degree of objectivity when we can also claim a degree of shared understanding. When Polonius agreed with Hamlet that 'yonder cloud' was 'like a camel', the effect was immediately spoilt by having to agree that it was also 'like a weasel' and 'very like a whale'. Were they seeing the same thing? To suppose that each solitary individual can only finally depend on his own insights is to be led into the kind of impasse in which some parts of our own culture now find themselves. As a science-based culture, it makes great claims to objectivity. But in so far as it is built on a philosophy of the isolated individual, the claim to objectivity is being steadily eroded. Many people talk happily about 'my truth' or 'your truth', but shy away from awkward questions about whether there is any such thing as 'the truth' to which they might approximate.

Something has gone seriously wrong. But para-doxically, alongside this individualistic entrapment there is a strong popular commitment to the idea that persons are valuable, and should be treated as such, and that we should not be limited in our concern simply to our own kind. I suspect that most readers of this book feel deeply about the plight of people in remote parts of the world, people they have never met, and are never likely to meet, but who may be facing disasters, poverty, or oppression. We are reminded daily that we are one world, and that we are responsible for one another. Yet there may also be an uncomfortable awareness that such sentiments are hard to justify if the world really is just a battleground between isolated individuals with selfish genes, and if moral commitment has somehow to be extracted from individualistic beliefs which leave no room for it. Persons are valuable, but if our intellectual assumptions about what persons are contradict our feelings of oneness and sympathy for them, something has to give – and it could be our moral concern.

Determinism and free will

The difficulty is focused for some people in doubts over whether we really have any choice in such matters. There is a nagging suspicion that when all has been said about the limitations of the mechanistic view of the world, as propounded by Descartes, and about the unique qualities of the human mind, it is still hard to find a rational place in the scheme of things for the notion of free will. How is it possible to make sense of what seem like arbitrary interruptions into the otherwise orderly course of events? Determinism has a strong intellectual appeal, because scientific advances seem constantly to confirm it. The truth is, of course, that far from being a scientific discovery, it is one of science's underlying assumptions. Scientists find causal connections because that is what they are looking for. The more successful the search, the easier it is to conclude that no other types of explanation are valid.

It also has to be admitted that free will is a difficult concept. Even St Augustine found himself in a tangle over it. Having asserted its existence on the basis of his own inner exploration, and having opened up a way of thinking which focused on the experiencing and freely active 'I' as the core of personality, he then had to deny free will in order to make sense of his further claim that human choice is entirely dependent on God's grace. The more he stressed God's initiative and foreknowledge as the only ground for salvation, the more the horrors of predestination reared their head.

Descartes, on the other hand, could assert the existence of free will, despite his belief in a mechanical universe, since the mind as he conceived it was a different kind of reality from the body, and therefore not subject to the same deterministic laws.

Kant and his successors took this independence of the will even further in stressing its primacy as the basis of morality, indeed to the point at which the will was virtually identified with the person. But since the essence of being a person in Kant's eyes was rationality, the true exercise of the will had to be rational – in other words, the very opposite of arbitrary choice.

How this rational will operated in a deterministic

world was just as much a problem for Kant as the mode of interaction between mind and matter was for Descartes, but it was less obvious because rational behaviour would, on the face of it, appear to conform to the way the world actually is. In our own day, despite the strong reactions against Enlightenment thinking, there is a widespread feeling that determinism might be true, even among those who know nothing about the technical discussions. At the root of it is the awareness that we are always learning more about ourselves, and the way we function, and the multifarious influences – physical, social, psychological, economic, and so forth – which impinge on us when we make our decisions. So why assume that this knowledge will suddenly reach an impassable barrier?

Nevertheless, as I shall argue in the next chapter when describing 'web theory', and in Chapter 12 when considering the implications of genetics, the notion of causality is not as simple as it may seem. Though we may analyse and come to understand in retrospect the choices made by other people, there is a deep implausibility about regarding our own choices as predetermined. When something has actually happened, the various causes which contributed to it are, as it were, laid out on the table and can be evaluated in their relationship to one another. Before it has happened, particularly in complex and delicately balanced systems, it may be impossible to tell which causal factors are going to predominate. This is one of the basic insights underlying chaos theory, best known for its application to weather forecasting and the much quoted 'butterfly effect', whereby small and unpredictable perturbations may have enormous consequences. It may also have applications to that complex and delicately balanced system, the human brain. According to this model, our choices may well be explicable, indeed if we are claiming that they are sensible choices we might hope that they were, but this is not the same as claiming that they were predictable. The most creative choices are both sensible and surprising.

There is no need to appeal to a still controversial theory, however, to establish the distinction between explicability and predictability. The difference between explaining the behaviour of individuals in terms of their character, and explaining it away as the inevitable consequence of impersonal forces, is crucial within ordinary human relationships. The delinquent youths in *West Side Story* may have been able to rattle off a list of social deprivations as the explanation for their behaviour, but they were rightly given no truck by the police sergeant who had heard it all before. To claim that one is not responsible for one's actions is to contract out of the business of being a person.

At this stage in the argument it is perhaps enough to point out that to believe in free will is not to claim that our actions are arbitrary, but is to locate them in those processes of attention, reflection, evaluation, conversation and interaction between minds which I have begun to explore in this chapter. Free will cannot ultimately be described as a kind of mechanism, in which context it is rightly seen as a contradiction in terms, despite the loophole offered by chaos theory.

It belongs within a different kind of story we need to tell about ourselves, a specifically personal one. It is a feature of that open-endedness which, as we shall see later, is one of our most distinctive human characteristics. The relationship between the scientific story and the personal one will be explored in later chapters. At this stage it is sufficient to say that both are needed.

My rapid historical survey in the last three chapters has so far brought us full circle. I have tried to show the rich potential in the concept of 'person' as represented in trinitarian theology. I have made the point that this holds together the notions of distinctiveness, relationship between persons, and the substantial reality of personhood as finding its image in the reality of God. I have described how this is not where our culture is now. Too great an emphasis on the division between inward and outward reality has made inwardness seem more and more insubstantial. Too great an emphasis on persons as rational, autonomous individuals has obscured our essential relatedness to one another, without which we would not be rational at all. It is hardly surprising that, as moral philosophers have grappled with the question of why we should place such high value on persons, they have found no adequate replacement for the ancient belief that personal worth is somehow based on being made in the image of God.

Before trying to defend in more detail a theologically based understanding of what persons are, I must describe a further step in the direction of disintegration, one which takes to extreme limits the kind of open-endedness I have been describing as the basis of free will.

6

Disintegration

Barry is trying to seduce Julia over the Internet. They are participants in a computer game, responding to the role, or persona, which each has adopted. As is customary in such games, the people playing them are anonymous, and the characters they have chosen may bear little or no relation to what they are like in real life. The action takes place in imaginary rooms, houses, or castles, constructed on the Internet site, and furnished in loving detail by the players themselves. For those who play such games for many hours a day, these imaginary rooms may serve as substitute homes, so involved do the players become. Communication takes place through typing instructions and conversations on a computer keyboard. Games can go on for months or years, and complex relationships can develop. A computer seduction can be as emotionally demanding as if it were happening in reality. Indeed, for the addict, participation in one or more of these Multi-User-Domains – MUDs for short – may be more satisfying than Real Life, which shrinks to RL. In a bad case of addiction, RL can shrink so far as to seem merely one aspect of a multiple identity – and not the most interesting one at that. It is perhaps significant that the D in MUDs used to stand for Dungeons, a reminder that the origin of this whole extraordinary set-up lay in fantasy board games.

Garrett, a twenty-eight-year-old male computer programmer, adopted the role of a helpful female frog called Ribbit for over a year, and in so doing found himself more free to express the non-competitive aspects of his character, which had hitherto been repressed. Stewart, a shy, antisocial physics graduate, chose to play using a highly sociable and desirable persona, which he named Achilles; but in the end he decided that the whole thing had been 'an addictive waste of time'. Barry's seduction was not a success. He failed to spot that in real life 'Julia' was nothing more than a computer programme.

This is the bizarre world we find in a recent book called *Life on the Screen* by Sherry Turkle, an academic psychologist working among students in the Massachusetts Institute of Technology. From her descriptions it would seem that most of the students had some hefty personal problems and that the MUDs, in which they lived a substantial part of their lives, provided either an escape, or a potential means of discovering repressed aspects of their personalities. Some seemed to benefit. Some found that by going online they could experience a sense of community which had never been theirs in real life. Others were given a licence to irresponsibility, and discovered that the pain caused to fellow participants in virtual reality could sometimes be just as severe as if they had been reacting face to face. Today's children with their Japanese computer pets, who are deeply upset when their pets 'die', seem likely candidates for tomorrow's MUDs.

Reality in such a world is what we make it to be. So is the person. The idea that there might be multiple selves living in multiple worlds no longer seems strange to those who have found new identities through the almost limitless imaginative powers now at their disposal. The difference between this concept of what it is to be a person, and the picture of the isolated, rational individual observing a mechanistic world, as described in the previous chapter, is a measure of the changes which have taken place in the last three hundred years.

It is not that people have never played roles or indulged in fantasies before. The word 'person' acquired its first meaning in precisely such circumstances. People have always imagined different worlds and experimented with alternative identities. Actors make a profession of it. Readers and television watchers are nourished by the personalities of their heroes. Gender swapping has a respectable history in Shakespeare. Children use fantasy to discover themselves. Alice down the rabbit hole wondered who she was and 'began thinking over all the children she knew that were of the same age as herself, to see if she could have been changed for any of them'. I distinctly remember a long period I spent as captain of a pirate ship at the age of four, and how I lived the part with an exaggerated limp. But I also knew when it was time for tea, and the line between fantasy and reality was never in doubt.

It is no longer easy to be so certain. The new powers of simulation and communication have created new possibilities of excess. The frontier between the real and the simulated has in some contexts been so effectively blurred, that Disneyland comes to be regarded as the 'real' America. It is not uncommon for Internet addicts to think of themselves as fragmented into a 'pastiche of personalities', belonging to separate, unrelated worlds in which they are quite literally 'different people'. This splitting of personalities goes far beyond the separation between such customary roles as parent, worker, pub-goer, football fan and so forth, which people generally manage to hold together without loss of identity. In the real world, though not in fantasy worlds, the different roles inescapably overlap.

There is more to the change of perception I am seeking to describe than just the extravagant use of technological gadgets. Gadgetry can create the opportunities, but the eagerness with which the opportunities are seized is symptomatic of a far deeper shift in self-understanding. The Internet has been described as postmodernism in action. It symbolises a new outlook on life, in its freedom from control, its repudiation of authority, its diversity of input, its invitation to imaginative indulgence, its speed, and its superficiality. Outside its serious uses as a source of almost unlimited information, it can feed attitudes which have arisen from the widespread sense of disillusionment with the ordered, mechanistic world bequeathed by Descartes and his successors. Against the dead hand of scientific materialism, and the isolation of the individual mind, surfing the Internet can give substance to the belief that there is no single 'right' view of the world, just an endless variety of experiences, opinions, feelings. The vistas opened up invite us to create our own world, and a new persona for ourselves in whatever image we prefer. The irony that the postmodernist revolt should find such perfect expression in one of the modern world's most sophisticated technological products is often lost on those who talk most loudly about the new spiritual freedom.

Romanticism

The beginnings of the revolt are to be found in the Romantic movement of the late eighteenth and early nineteenth centuries. If the world was mere mechanism, and if the rational mind had to be content with clear, hard, rigidly defined ideas, then there must be other ways of expressing the real experience of being a person. Poetry may get nearer to the truth than philosophy. Artists may be able to convey insights for which there are as yet no words. The idea that we may in some sense be able to create our own world is not new; it is what the artistic imagination has always been doing. Sensitive spirits can create spheres of meaning which go beyond mere individualistic self-expression and give shared insight into the depths of human feeling. When Wordsworth felt

> A presence that disturbs me with the joy
> Of elevated thoughts; a sense sublime

Of something far more deeply interfused,
Whose dwelling is the light of setting suns,
And the round ocean and the living air,
And the blue sky, and in the mind of man.
('Lines composed a few miles above Tintern
Abbey', 1798)

he was able to put into words what millions of other people have dimly sensed, but not brought to conscious awareness until the words were there to help them.

Mary Shelley's *Frankenstein* is a classic expression both of the romantic revolt against the arrogance of mechanistic science, and of fears about where it might lead. Frankenstein's aim was to 'explore unknown powers, and unfold to the world the deepest mysteries of creation', an achievement from which he was eventually to recoil in horror. It is significant that Mary Shelley locates the immediate cause of his creature's murderous career in its misery at its aloneness. 'I am malicious because I am miserable. Am I not shunned and hated by all mankind? [mainly, in the first instance, on account of its hideous appearance] You, my creator, would tear me to pieces, and triumph; remember that, and tell me why I should pity man more than he pities me.' She correctly diagnosed that it is not just scientific hubris which humanity should fear, but the glacial awareness of isolation which its philosophy might engender.

Lewis Carroll, in a very different mode, created worlds in which children could begin to understand themselves and come to terms with their fears and frustrations. He was himself the product of an exaggeratedly formal age, locked into the rigid social patterns of Victorian England with its emphasis on manners and propriety. The strange world in which Alice finds herself is one which carries formality to an absurd degree, so much so that its manners deserve to be mocked rather than respected. 'Look up, speak nicely, and don't twiddle your fingers all the time,' said the Red Queen, once described as the concentrated essence of governesses. 'Curtsey while you're thinking what to say. It saves time.' Later, at her feast, Alice is first introduced to a leg of mutton, and then told, 'It isn't etiquette to cut anyone you have been introduced to.' This is liberating language. Carroll was creating for his child readers a world in which nonsense can be seen as nonsense, so that its adult equivalent need no longer be feared.

When contrasting Carroll with Kafka in Chapter 1, my aim was to show how the creative imagination could be far from liberating, could indeed be menacing and, in Kafka's case, a sinister foretaste of what was to come. In Kafka's world, to be alive is at the same time to be under sentence of death. In *The Trial* K. is obsessed by awareness of another world which is inaccessible to him. His own experience is like that of an eavesdropper, knowing that matters of high importance are afoot, but able only to catch an indistinct whisper of what is being said. He is always, frustratingly, on the edge of understanding, though never attaining it. He lives in a modern city, busy with its own affairs and ghostlike in its indeterminateness. He remains, like Frankenstein's rejected creature, fundamentally alone, imprisoned by guilt, simply for being what he is. Mid-twentieth-century Jews were to experience such a world at first hand. Their late-twentieth-century Gentile counterparts are more likely to say, 'What the hell!' and rob a bank for their next fix.

Nietzsche

Friedrich Nietzsche too, misunderstood and largely ignored in his own day, was a sign of things to come. He illustrates what could happen to personal self-understanding under the influence of a powerfully critical and destructive imagination, and has been the major inspiration behind the various forms of twentieth-century nihilism. Later radical thinkers, like Michel Foucault, worked to the agenda set by him, in particular the constant reinvention of himself, the advice to live dangerously, and a suspicion of knowledge as always and inevitably tainted by being part of a power game.

Nietzsche marks the culmination of the belief that the isolated self, identified by him exclusively as the human will, is the sole criterion of what is true or right. 'Active successful natures act, not according to the dictum "know thyself", but as if there hovered before them the commandment: *will* a self and thou shalt *become* a self . . .' he wrote. The only real man, in other words, is self-created, and the only truth is what a self-created man perceives to be true. His favourite description of himself was as a 'free spirit', looking down from a great height on the bumblings of previous philosophers. Real philosophers 'create values', they are 'commanders and law-givers', 'their "knowing" is creating, their creating is a law-giving, their will to truth is – will to power.'

There is nothing absolute about science, according to Nietzsche. The ordered mechanistic world, so carefully mapped by the scientific disciples of Descartes, may pass muster for the time being. But 'it is perhaps just dawning on five or six minds that physics too is only an interpretation and arrangement of the world . . . and *not* an explanation of the world.' In this he spoke more truly than he knew; the replacement of Newtonian physics by relativity and quantum theory was still more than twenty years in the future. He saw that truth evolves and changes; but he went too far in concluding from this that 'nothing is true'; and even further in his assertion that, if nothing is true, 'everything is permitted'. Morality, like truth, collapses in a world in which the only power is that of the will. The ripest fruit of the history of morals is 'the sovereign individual, equal only to himself, all moral custom left far behind'.

Nietzsche is an extreme example, but he is interesting for my purposes because he illustrates the connection between a highly constricted view of a person as an isolated will, and a highly sceptical view of objective reality. If the power of choice is paramount, then the difference between real life and virtual reality becomes more and more problematic. We can make our world in our own image. It is the same deadly combination which has reappeared in fancy dress in postmodernism, but without such arrogance or such destructive overtones. Postmodernism replays Nietzschean tragedy as farce.

Fortunately most people are neither Nietzscheans nor postmodernists. Many are simply bewildered and disorientated by the multiplicity of competing ideas, and worried by the destruction of many of the landmarks, both intellectual and moral, which once gave their lives security and meaning. They do not play games on the Internet, but cannot escape exposure to the constant barrage of new ideas and experiences. Television in particular, with its kaleidoscopic quality and its rapid turnover of images and themes, mirrors the kind of world in which there is no fixed reality, but an overwhelming surfeit of opinions. In a Nietzschean mood one might see a television remote control as symbolising the power of choice held by the solitary viewer. The difference is that the viewer is passive, the power is exceedingly limited, and the version of reality encountered, far from being created by the self, is fed to it by others. We live in unheroic times in which the posturings of a Nietzsche can seem absurd. The bewilderment and the sense of disintegration are genuine, however, and that is why it is important to see where it might all end for those who go too far down the road he explored.

To be a free spirit seems wonderfully appealing, until the exercise of freedom begins to erode the confidence that we are persons dealing with other persons who have a reality equal to our own, and that there is a givenness about our common personhood which deserves respect. Nor is it only persons who have this quality of givenness. The world of nature remains obstinately what it is: To master it by our 'will to power' was once an ideal – think of all the talk of 'conquering' mountains and 'taming' nature – but is now beginning to look increasingly shabby and dangerous; nature too deserves respect. Though it is certainly possible to invent alternative worlds, they remain fantasies. If there is to be a successful release from this impasse, a protection against the disintegration of personhood in a mechanistic world, we will have to look elsewhere for it.

Relatedness

The most hopeful counterpoise to the tendencies I have been describing is the traditional insight that persons exist essentially in relationship. This was a theme already implicit in the original concept of 'person' as role. It was given new depth by trinitarian theology, especially in the Eastern tradition. It was subsequently overshadowed by increasing emphasis on the person as an individual soul, and latterly as an individual will. It only began to resurface in the late nineteenth century, particularly through the writings of Hegel, with the realisation that human beings cannot be understood outside their social context.

The key significance of relatedness was expressed powerfully and succinctly by John Macmurray in his 1954 Gifford Lectures:

We need one another to be ourselves. This

complete and unlimited dependence of each of us upon the others is the central and crucial fact of personal existence. Individual independence is an illusion; and the independent individual, the isolated self, is a nonentity. In ourselves we are nothing; and when we turn our eyes inward in search of ourselves we find a vacuum ... It is only in relation to others that we exist as persons; we are invested with significance by others who have need of us; and we borrow our reality from those who care for us. We live and move and have our being not in ourselves but in one another; and what rights or powers or freedom we possess are ours by the grace and favour of our fellows. Here is the basic fact of our human condition ...

The truth and importance of this will, I hope, become apparent later on, as we look at the formation of human personality through the kind of interactions which language and other modes of human contact make possible. Here, however, I am concerned only to note the need for caution. Just as a one-sided emphasis on the individual can be destructive, so a concept of personality entirely dependent on relatedness can in the end dissolve individual personal substance into nothingness. There are people haunted by the idea that they are no more than the point of intersection of other people's influence on them, that what they call their personality is indeed, as John Macmurray hints, nothing more than a vacuum, shaped by its boundaries, but having no content. There is a parallel with my earlier description of the isolated individual as no more than the seeing eye where the lines of sight converge.

It could be said in favour of the participants in MUDs is that at least they seem to have been working on the principle that they need other people in order to discover themselves. The fact that they made contact only at second hand through an assumed persona suggests that they were nevertheless hiding themselves from real encounter, and were therefore unlikely to escape from their isolation except in fantasy. There are other stories of Internet communities which have generated quite a different quality of relatedness, particularly among isolated people looking for conversation partners. The point is that it is not the computer screen as such, or the telephone, or any other device, which determines the significance of communication, but the degree to which those involved give their real selves to each other. That requires a consciousness of being a self outside the relationship, and hence of having something to give.

In the early 1950s a sociological study of the changing American character attracted wide attention, but now seems almost forgotten. The authors of *The Lonely Crowd* drew a distinction between three types of character, 'tradition-directed', 'inner-directed', and 'other-directed'. Tradition-directed people belong within close-knit communities and conform to their community's cultural ethos, which by and large is fixed, comprehensive and monochrome. Most ancient, non-urban communities were tradition-directed in this sense, as was most of medieval society. Inner-directed people have strongly internalised the values of their parents or community, and have thus in a measure become independent of them; they have their own powerful psychic gyroscope. These are the sturdy, isolated individuals, confident of being able to exercise their will, Puritans and Protestants – the true American pioneers. Other-directed people, by contrast, are no longer members of the traditional kind of community which provides them with clear signals about behaviour, nor do they have the inner capacity to go it alone. They pick up signals from all and sundry and are always ready to change; they are cosmopolitan, at home everywhere and nowhere, capable of rapid (if sometimes superficial) intimacy with, and response to, everyone. They know what they like, even if they do not know what they really want. Sincerity, or at least the appearance of it, is the most highly prized virtue. The contrast between inner- and other-direction is neatly summed up in an alternative version of an old nursery rhyme:

> This little pig went to market;
> This little pig stayed at home.
> This little pig had roast beef;
> This little pig had none.
> This little pig went wee-wee-wee
> All the way home.

The rhyme, say the authors, may be taken as a paradigm of individuation and unsocialised behaviour among children of an earlier age. Today, however, all little pigs go to market; none stays at home; all have roast beef, if any do; and all say wee-wee-wee.

The other-directed character is strong on relationships, but lacks the solid centre of old-style inner-direction. A further step down this road is described by another American author, Larry Rasmussen, writing forty years later. In *Moral Fragments and Moral Community* he writes:

> We can often speak eloquently of our needs, desires and feelings; but we lack utterly the language of moral formation, obligation, and public commitment. Why? ... because the therapeutic mentality has triumphed in such degree among middle Americans that there is no goal to our discourse beyond the process itself ... We crave intimacy itself as community but there is no ethic here beyond 'listening'. Nonjudgmental openness is prized, conflict and guilt are shunned. Warmth is our god. (p. 105)

He quotes a cartoon which shows a smiling viewer listening attentively as the television announces: 'It's the Small-Town Life Soap Opera Network, giving you the security of community ties without the risk of personal human contact' (p. 107).

Relatedness, in other words, can be a sham unless it is rooted in something deeper than sociability. I have cited these American examples because they illustrate the pitfalls in reacting so strongly against individualism that the making of relationships becomes the be-all and end-all of being a person. We need to *be* something before we can properly relate. But the converse is also true, that we can only become something in so far as we *do* relate to others. What that something is will be the subject of later chapters, in the further exploration of how personal identity is actually formed. As I see it, all three directions described in *The Lonely Crowd* are important for the development of a mature personality. We need the confidence and security of being rooted in a tradition, the strength which comes from the possession of clear, internalised values, and the breadth and receptivity entailed in being responsive to others.

The potential misunderstandings are well illustrated in a British context by the largely abortive disputes between politicians and church leaders during the Thatcher era. Mrs Thatcher wanted to encourage individualism, in the shape of individual enterprise, which she saw as the only answer to the kind of dependency created by the collectivist policies of previous administrations. Individualism and collectivism were for her the two opposite poles, and when she made her famous remark about there being 'no such thing as society', she presumably had this contrast in mind. Only a collectivist society has the ability to change the conditions of peoples' lives without relying on the enterprise and initiative of the individuals who compose it.

Church leaders, in attacking her individualism, were not proposing collectivism as an alternative, but wanted to stress more than she did the extent to which individuals are shaped by the society in which they live. They were making the point that the quality of a society is an important factor in the process of its members becoming responsible and self-reliant people. The point was repeatedly ignored or misunderstood, because the emphasis placed by Christian representatives on the importance of community could be misinterpreted as a harking back to the kind of tradition-centred community from which enterprising individuals had had to make their escape. Frequent references to the destruction of mining communities, as coal mines were closed, underlined this impression. In short, there was confusion on both sides, through a failure to reach any common understanding of the kinds of relatedness which are significant for human flourishing, and the kind of public commitments by individuals and governments which are necessary to bring this about.

There is a more general and deeper source of confusion in the modern world which will ensure that the arguments continue. It lies in the multitude of conflicting messages about what it is to be a human being, and about what kind of society it is in which we live. I have already referred to the contribution made by television to this confusion, as it swamps viewers with a succession of mostly superficial images. A severe critic, Steven Connor, has also described, in his book *Postmodernist Culture*, how it threatens to abolish the distinction between the private and the public.

> Just as the private worlds of actual individuals are relentlessly pillaged by TV, with the multiplication of intimate explorations of private lives and fly-on-the-wall documentaries, so the private world comes to enfold or be inhabited by the public world of historical events, which are made

available instantly in every living-room by the agency of TV. The public possesses the private, the private encompasses the public. What typifies this situation above all is an explosion of visibility... (p. 169)

It remains to be seen whether the greatly increased power of choice, as television channels multiply, will tend to restore individual integrity and respect for persons, or simply add to the confusion. The omens are not promising. If superficiality triumphs and the 'explosion of visibility' is taken to its extreme, there is a danger of further diminishing the possibilities of authentic relatedness, and weakening the consciousness of being a private inner self. We could find ourselves living in a society as vacuous as that depicted in *Hello!* magazine.

Thinking in webs

Fortunately there are contrary tendencies. A relatively new way of thinking, which takes seriously the multiformity of experience, the creative role of the individual, and our essential inter-relatedness, makes use of the concept of webs or networks. Dynamic modern societies are no longer hierarchical, but depend on a complex network of lateral relationships. The most successful large businesses are those where authority is most dispersed, and where there is plenty of scope for individual initiative. The structural plan of the motorcar industry, for instance, would reveal an enormous diversity of small firms and operating units, co-ordinated but not controlled by a relatively small central organisation.

Government has to operate in the same way. As the collapse of the Communist command economies has shown, modern economic processes and structures are far too complex for any one group of people to be able to make effective plans about how they should work. Capitalism is a form of dis-integration, a dispersal of the decision-making capacity. So, in theory, is democracy. But democracy, if it is to work, needs dispersal through a multitude of local organisations and associations in which people learn to take responsibility for different aspects of their lives. This web of freely chosen commitments and responsibilities in what is now called 'civil society' is increasingly recognised as the basis of a free society. The lack of it in many former Eastern-bloc states has been a prime reason for the slow and uncertain growth of effective democracy there.

I have recently had personal experience of the complex inter-relationships necessary at government level through chairing a government committee set up to study and advise on the possibilities of transplanting animal organs into human patients. This relatively modest committee has to relate to some fifteen other bodies, statutory and non-statutory, all of which have some interest or expertise in the work it is charged to do. The development of lateral links, the exchange of appropriate information and the sharing of expertise are essential to its function, and all this is only a tiny fragment of the vast network of individuals, groups, committees, trusts and other bodies, which together constitute the National Health Service. The Secretary of State for Health may have to look as if he is controlling it, and may indeed have to make some crucial decisions, but networks mostly have to function by inter-relationship between the parts, rather than by dictates from above.

The concept of webs and networks has also become familiar through the study of ecology. Countless books and television programmes have hammered home the point that in the world of nature, everything depends on everything else. Use insecticides on your crops, and you may also destroy the bird population. Cut down a rain forest, and you may eradicate hundreds of species dependent on the specialised environmental niches which only that complex living system provided. Be careless with CFCs, and you may destroy the habitat of the Antarctic penguins. Life itself is a monster web, of which human beings are a part. We are a peculiarly dangerous section of the web, because we alone among living things have the power to cause major disruptions within it by our own folly, ignorance, or greed.

Thinking in webs and networks also extends to reason itself. Traditional thinking about causation assumes the existence of chains of causes, such that A causes B, which causes C, and so on. The use of fossil fuels, we are told, causes excess carbon dioxide in the atmosphere, which causes global warming, which causes the peculiar weather which now seems increasingly common. That may seem like a straightforward chain of causes and effects, but the reality is much more complex, which is why there has been so much debate over whether global warming is real, and if so what its long-term consequences might be. The sea, for instance, is an enormous reservoir both for heat and for carbon dioxide. As more and more factors of this kind are taken into account, the once simple chain of cause and effect begins to grow branches, form loops, and be subject to unpredictable feedbacks. In fact, it begins to look more like a network.

Similar complexity lies beneath the surface when somebody is diagnosed, say, as carrying a suspicious gene which might entail a high risk of heart attack. It is also there beneath questions such as, what caused the Hillsborough disaster which left Tony Bland as one of its tragic victims? Does it make any sense in such circumstances to try to identify a single cause, or even the main one? The idea of causes as a chain gained its plausibility from the simplest examples of direct causation, such as when I knock a vase, it falls over and breaks. But most real-life situations are not like that. Things happen for multiple reasons, and it is usually the coincidence of different factors, rather than a single identifiable cause, which determines the result. Whether I have a heart attack may be influenced by my genetic make-up, but it will also be influenced by my lifestyle, my circumstances, and sometimes by sheer luck. To think of causes as part of a web of predispositions or influences is to see the gross limitations of any view of the world as some kind of vast machine. Causation in machines usually is of the 'knock over the vase and watch it break' variety; but these instances are the exception rather than the rule, especially in the world of living things.

A similarly fruitful application of web thinking occurs when considering what it means to know something or to have it explained. People sometimes talk about the foundations of knowledge, as if one could start from some universally agreed propositions and slowly build up a great edifice of knowledge on this unshakable basis. This is what Descartes thought he was doing when he decided on the one thing he could not doubt – the fact that he was thinking. Christians on the whole have tended to think of their faith as based on 'the foundation of Scripture', as if all necessary Christian knowledge is already implicit in the Bible and simply has to be elucidated. Such ways of thinking seem more and more implausible nowadays. Nobody, in fact, learns like this. The process of learning is more like an endless series of feedbacks. We begin with ideas, assumptions, prejudices, scraps of experience, etc., into which we fit new knowledge, and this feeds back to modify our initial assumptions, which in turn dictate the kind of knowledge we seek, and so on ad infinitum.

Scientific knowledge, for instance, may look back to some foundational discoveries, but in fact the main ideas emerged slowly, bit by bit, and with many false starts and setbacks. Ideas which stood the test of time were gradually built into a network, and were frequently seen to be vindicated by the light they threw on other parts of the total structure. Ideas which had many connections within the network were more resistant to change than those which affected only a small area of knowledge. It is much easier, for example, to amend or even abandon one's ideas about the evolution of a single species than to doubt evolution itself. To doubt the latter would be to tear the heart out of the whole of modern biology. The picture, in other words, is that of a web in which lines converge around centrally important theories, and in which phenomena are 'explained' by being assigned a place within the system. We understand things by connecting them with one another.

The same is true of Christian understanding. To treat the Bible as the foundation of faith usually means in practice allowing it to illuminate and correct present Christian experience and thought. The description of it as the Church's book not only points to its origins in Christian experience, but is a reminder that the way it is read depends on context, and on the insights of countless believers who have studied it throughout Christian history. Insights derived from it are always part of a web of knowledge which, like scientific knowledge, has well-winnowed truths at the centre, and much room for exploration, growth and reconstruction at the periphery. St Paul's image of church members being like the limbs of a single body is a further instance of network thinking in a Christian context. Relatedness to one another is as essential for Christian existence as relatedness to God the Father, through Christ, and in the Spirit. The Holy Trinity is the most comprehensive web of all.

I hope I have said enough to show that the idea of webs and networks is a potentially fruitful one. There is a danger, in fact, that it may become too fashionable. All sorts of people these days seem keen on 'networking' – including 'Internetworking'. If sensibly handled, however, thinking in webs can help to capture the sense of being multiply related to one another, and being subject to multiple experiences, even at times being multiple selves, without the descent into chaos and arbitrariness which some expressions of post-modernism seem to threaten. A network is not infinitely flexible. It provides a place for things, but a place which is always connected to other things. This making of connections is closely allied to what we describe as 'giving a meaning to things'. Thinking in webs can also act as a corrective to Descartes by exposing the unreality of his solitary thinker, and by countering his mechanistic bias. It is a reminder that thinking is not quite the logical progression it is sometimes made out to be. Nor does a world in which it is possible to identify causes necessarily have to be deterministic. Multiple causation implies that we never really know when we have reached the final explanation.

So what does it tell us about being a person? To think of myself as part of a whole seems to be nearer the truth than to suppose that I am an isolated individual – particularly one who wonders whether other minds exist. Suppose, however, that the whole of which I am part is no more than a less mechanised version of the world of objects as conceived by Descartes. Would this radically alter my sense of being a person? This is the question to which I turn in the next chapter.

7

Minds and brains

The American philosopher Daniel Dennett, in his ambitiously titled book *Consciousness Explained*, records the curious case of a Frenchman who in 1800 fell into what he called:

> a true delirium brought on by the terrors of the revolution . . . he believed that he was guillotined, and his head thrown pell-mell onto the pile of the other victims' heads, and that the judges, repenting too late of their cruel deed, had ordered the heads to be taken and rejoined to their respective bodies. However, by an error of some sort, they put his head on the shoulders of another unfortunate. This idea that his head had been changed occupied him night and day . . . 'See my teeth!' he would repeat incessantly, 'they used to be wonderful, and these are rotten! My mouth was healthy, and this one's infected! What a difference between this hair and the hair I had before my change of head!' (p. 106, footnote)

Part of the fascination of the story lies in the way the victim of this delusion identifies himself with his body, rather than with his head. The instinctive reaction is to do just the opposite. There are numerous science fiction stories in which isolated heads are somehow kept alive and function as if they were people. Enthusiasts who arrange for the preservation of their bodies after death by freezing, in the hope that at some future date a cure for whatever killed them might be found, are equally happy to settle for the preservation of their heads (a cheaper option), or just their brains (presumably even cheaper). Most people, if asked to locate their 'self', would probably think of a point just behind their eyes, before realising that it is rather foolish to imagine locating it at all.

A head and two legs

There are good reasons why heads feature so prominently in our conception of ourselves. The ground plan of all vertebrates (and many non-vertebrates too) includes a head of some kind where the so-called special senses – vision, hearing, taste and smell – are clustered. Apart from the sense of touch, which needs to be distributed all over the body, these constitute the main sensory input to the brain. It is therefore natural to think of ourselves as being where that input is concentrated.

There are biological advantages in this concentration. It enables the myriad of nerve fibres connecting the sense organs with the brain to be kept short, and the different forms of input to be more easily co-ordinated. The nerve impulses which carry this input travel fast, but not so fast as to make the distance between the sense receptors and the brain irrelevant. Since the rate of conduction depends on temperature, the problem of co-ordination is greater in reptiles than in mammals, and long reptiles run the risk of delayed responses when the external temperature is low. There is a nice prehistoric example of this problem in the largest of the dinosaurs, the thirty-yard-long diplodocus. If, as generally supposed, it was cold-blooded, it could easily have had the end of its tail bitten off on a frosty morning before any warning signal reached its head. Perhaps this is why it developed a modest secondary brain at the base of its spine, thus achieving a unique capacity to think a priori and a posteriori simultaneously.

The fact that vertebrates also feed and breathe through their heads complicates the picture, though there are good reasons why the mouth should be in close proximity to the special senses. Four-legged animals which move horizontally need both to observe and to forage at the front end. The sense of smell, in particular, depends on breathing, and in most mammals is the main sense used in foraging. There is a further advantage for four-legged animals in that the positioning of their teeth and jaws in their heads makes it possible to use them as offensive weapons.

The downside of all this is that strong jaws and horizontal heads need thick skulls to which to attach powerful muscles. The thickness of the skull limits the size of the brain. Since brains are heavy, the larger the brain in a horizontal head, the more massive the neck muscles required to support it, which in turn require an even thicker skull to which to attach themselves, which in turn increases the weight, thus necessitating stronger muscles, and so on. Given this vicious circle, it is not hard to see why the ability to stand and walk upright was such a crucial development in the evolution of human beings. In the upright posture the head can balance on the top of the spine, which bears its weight, thereby reducing the need for a thick skull and large neck muscles, and setting the vicious circle in reverse – hence the possibility of larger brains. It is only when we try to move horizontally, as when crawling on all fours, or trying to lift our head from a prone position, that we notice how inadequate our neck muscles really are to support its full weight for any length of time.

Furthermore, standing upright frees the front limbs to act as arms and hands, and this in turn frees the mouth from having to be used as a weapon. Strong jaw muscles, with heavy ridges on the skull to anchor them, are no longer so necessary, thus leaving still more room for the brain. The new position of the skull in relation to the spinal column also leaves more room for the larynx, which in apes is relatively narrow and pushed towards the back of the throat. A larger and more flexible larynx greatly increases the range of sounds which can be made, and thus opens up the possibility of speech. Likewise the fact that the hands no longer have to be used in locomotion opens up the possibility of their becoming precision instruments which, like the ability to use complex speech, still further increases the desirability and advantages of possessing a more powerful brain to control them.

The upright posture also carries penalties. Human beings are especially vulnerable to choking, given our vertical windpipe and the forward position of the larynx, which brings its entrance dangerously close to the oesophagus. The use of only two legs for walking also poses some mechanical problems. If we are to do so without swaying awkwardly from side to side, our legs need to be positioned relatively close together. To be reasonably agile, therefore, human beings cannot afford to have too large a pelvis, and this places a severe restriction on the size of an infant's head at the time of birth. This is one reason why, in contrast with most other mammals, human birth can be a difficult and dangerous procedure, and why babies are born with their brains in a relatively undeveloped state.

The penalty of small birth size can be turned to advantage, however. Human babies may not be able to stand on their feet and run like newborn antelopes, and they are utterly incapable of surviving by themselves. But the fact of their total dependence on their parents, and the necessity for a long period of postnatal learning, sets the scene for much less reliance on instinctive behaviour, and much greater mental flexibility and resourcefulness in later life. It also undergirds the necessity for stable family life, and social arrangements which protect the young and support the learning process. With such a high premium on the transmission of experience from one generation to the next, it is not hard to see why tradition and culture are so important for human beings, and why over thousands of years structures have been developed to make this transmission possible and to promote it. These may seem large consequences to flow from the simple fact of standing upright, but in evolutionary terms the new possibilities created by this change of posture contained the seeds of most of what is distinctive about being human.

It is a compressed and complex story. To know its bare outline is to begin to understand some of the constraints our bodies impose on us. It can help us to make sense of the familiar illustrations showing our early human ancestors as forward-crouching, heavy-jawed, low-browed creatures, and to appreciate the significance of a million years of tiny alterations in the shape of our heads. It is also an example of how in the biological world everything is connected to everything else. A difference in posture, brought about by who knows what, perhaps simply by a change in climate, can trigger off a series of interlinked transformations which could not have been foreseen. Yet they have an underlying logic. It is possible to identify certain design features which belong together in large-brained, mentally flexible, agile and dexterous animals, and which give the lie to fantasies about intelligent creatures having been able to evolve into any shape whatever. Aliens from outer space, if they are going to feel comfortable on earth, must make the same concessions to the force of gravity that we do, and I must confess to some worries about the ability of ET's neck to support his head. Octopuses, squids and dolphins, which also have highly developed nervous systems, are not exceptions to this rule because, as aquatic animals, their shape and structure are not so dependent on gravity. Evolution may be driven by random variations, but it is not arbitrary in its outcomes. These are constrained, in the way I have tried to indicate, by the kind of world this is, and by the fact that one change inevitably triggers another.

Our brains are the product of these constraints, a vast, interacting network of nerve cells and nerve fibres, packed into a limited cavity and dominated, in the case of human beings, by the sense organs for sight and hearing, which are closest to it and provide the greatest input. Our consciousness seems to a large extent to take its flavour from these two senses. Though other information is constantly pouring into our brains, we tend to be consciously aware of it only when it comes with special urgency. There are receptors in our muscles, for instance, which monitor the position of our limbs, but though we can pay attention to all this information if we need to, or choose to, for the most part we do not. The same is true of our sense of touch. When cracking an old-fashioned combination safe, all attention, so I am told, is focused on the fingertips; but when we are watching a film, we may be scarcely conscious of our hands, and only conscious of other parts of our anatomy when we have been sitting on them for too long.

Many quite complicated responses, such as catching a ball or ducking to avoid a missile, can be processed in our brains without any conscious awareness of how we do it, or even whether we are going to do it. These may be acquired skills, or wired into our brains as part of our evolutionary inheritance. As we shall see later, any account of the evolution of the human mind is bound to be highly speculative. It is one thing to tell the story of the human head, and to try to deduce from this, and from comparative studies on animals, how the human brain might have evolved, but we have only the most fragmentary evidence of what might have been going on in prehuman minds. It seems fair to assume, however, that what we now regard as distinctive human capacities, including our present level of consciousness, developed slowly, just like our bodies, and to different degrees in different prehuman ancestors. On some interpretations of the fossil evidence, there have been a number of false starts, one of which is now assumed to be Neanderthal man. It follows that, whatever is meant by mind and consciousness, they are not all-or-nothing capacities, something a hominid either has or does not have, nor do mental phenomena necessarily accompany all brain activity. Some brain activity is conscious, in varying forms and to varying degrees. Much brain activity is not. Nor is it necessary to assume that consciousness is associated exclusively with activity in the cerebral cortex. There is evidence that at least some of our more primitive emotions have their seat in lower parts of the brain, the so-called limbic system. If so there are awkward questions about whether Tony Bland, who certainly could not think consciously or respond deliberately, might nevertheless have been able, in some very crude sense, to feel. But who or what would be experiencing the feeling, and how would one ever know?

Consciousness

Such questions plunge us right into the middle of one of the most disputed areas in the whole of science and philosophy. What *is* this mysterious thing we call consciousness? It is said that a new theory of consciousness is put forward roughly once a fortnight, an indication of the huge energy now being devoted to its study, and a sure sign that there is as yet no agreed way to tackle it and not much clarity about the precise issues.

All researchers agree that there must be a close relationship between the physical and chemical changes taking place in our brains and what we are conscious of experiencing and doing. A continuing theme of this book is the question of how one should interpret the significance of massive brain damage in trying to understand what is entailed in being a person. PVS is an extreme case, but there are plenty of less devastating forms of brain damage which raise similarly acute problems. Wide publicity was given a few years ago to the victim of a road accident, whose entire memory of his previous life had apparently been wiped out. He had to learn to speak again, walk again, perform the most elementary functions, and eventually married his wife again because he had no recollection either of her or their children. His wife referred to him as a different person, physically the same as the man she had married, but in every other respect a stranger. Whether the memory loss in his case will prove to be permanent or not remains to be seen, so the question of whether there really has been no continuity in his mental life remains unresolved. Nonetheless, there could hardly be a clearer case of the intimate relation between brain function and personality.

There are innumerable other instances of injury or disease affecting one or more personal characteristics, whether memory, perception, temperament, or skills. Sometimes the loss may be quite specific, such as a failure to recognise the meaning of words. Or there may just be a slow dissolution of personality, as in Alzheimer's disease, with occasional and increasingly rare glimpses of the previous personality. Most people have experience of the temporary changes of consciousness brought about by feeling depressed, or being drugged or intoxicated. There is no need to labour the point. Our immediate consciousness and our continuing personality have a physical basis, and are therefore vulnerable to physical changes.

There has been much interest in recent years in a newly discovered phenomenon called blindsight. It was first studied in a young man who had had part of his cerebral cortex removed to cure persistent migraine, and who then found that he was blind on one side of his visual field. It was noticed, however, that when he was asked to reach for something in this blind area he could do so almost as accurately as if he could see it. He would not spontaneously notice objects in his blind area, but would be aware of them if they were moving, in much the same way that a fish seems only to be attracted by movement. There is no problem in understanding how visual impulses were able to reach the young man's brain, because his eyes were functioning perfectly normally and there is a great deal of redundancy and crossing-over among the visual pathways in the brain. But the loss of part of his cortex had destroyed his ability consciously to see objects in certain positions, even though he could, when stimulated to do so, become in some obscure sense aware of them, by using some more primitive area of his brain. Consciousness and the ability to respond appropriately to a stimulus, in other words, do not necessarily coincide.

It is cases like this, and thousands of experiments based on less drastic conditions, which have revealed the complexity of the problems to be unravelled, as well as providing insight into how at least some parts of the brain do their work. One of the latest techniques, known as functional imaging, can detect the degree of activity in different areas of the brain by means of a continuous scan, and thus can correlate different mental processes with different brain locations. Psychological tests, computer modelling of neural networks and many other techniques and disciplines, including even quantum physics, have been called in to help build up as objective a picture as possible of how the brain works, and how its different parts relate to one another. But there is still a large question mark about whether, or how far, this massive amount of information and ingenious theorising can give an adequate account of what we actually experience as consciousness. Investigative studies of this kind inevitably treat consciousness as a kind of thing which can be viewed and understood from an external, objective point of view, whereas the essence of it, as actually experienced, is that it can only be known from the inside. It is about what it is to be me.

There is a deep divide between those who believe that an external, objective explanation is possible in principle and those who believe it is not. One version of this divide is between those who believe that there is only one kind of reality, and dualists who believe there are two. We have already met Descartes, the father of modern dualism, with his rigid distinction between inner mental experience and the external, machine-like world. I have referred to the inherent difficulty in seeing how these two kinds of reality could possibly interact. It is also the case that very few scientific investigators in this field will nowadays have anything to do with Cartesian dualism, their main reason being that it sets up an impassable barrier to further scientific exploration. If the explanation of some form of brain activity is that the person's soul has been tweaking the levers, science can say no more. Such a restriction on further exploration is ruled out by one of the basic articles of scientific belief, namely that there should in principle be no limits on the search for knowledge. The scientific map of reality contains no forbidden areas with the warning label, 'Here be dragons.' Whether it is the only map we need is another question altogether.

In view of this scientific belief, it is not surprising that in writing about consciousness many scientists and philosophers often display an extreme nervousness about anything which might even hint at the presence of some non-physical reality. Daniel Dennett, whom I have already quoted and whose theory I shall be commenting on later, is one of the most robust of the anti-dualists. He constantly rubs his readers' noses in the folly of saying 'here be miracles', and positively flaunts his materialism. He need not have worried. Not many philosophically minded theologians these days are dualists, and I have already sufficiently indicated, I hope, how disastrous the legacy of Descartes has been. It is not necessary to believe in a special kind of 'soul stuff' in order to recognise that reality, whatever we mean by the word, can be viewed from different perspectives; or to put the point another way, that for a complete account of our experience we have to tell different kinds of stories using different kinds of concepts. Stories about nerve impulses and stories about consciousness must in the end somehow relate to one another, but this does not mean that they are interchangeable. It makes no more sense to talk about, say, a red pattern of nerve impulses than about an electrical pattern of thought. To acknowledge this obvious fact enables us to identify the real gulf between those who would allow a theological perspective and those who would not. It is between those who believe that the whole story of mental activity can be reduced to a story about nerve impulses and chemical reactions, and those who believe that such radical reductionism ignores or obscures essential aspects of what we inwardly know.

The analogy with computers can be illuminating. Everything which happens inside a computer can be reduced to strings of figures in the form 0001011100110110, including what I am now writing. But I am also, I hope successfully, trying to convey a meaning, which will eventually be transmitted to you, the reader, through words in a book. As you read it, the information on the page will once again be converted into the equivalent of many strings of figures in your retina, ocular nerves and brain, because nerve impulses are a series of electrical pulses which are either on or off, just like the ones and noughts in a computer. Your perception of my meaning, however, will depend on a series of other factors which are not so easily codeable as letters in a book or impulses in nerves. In fact, the letters in the book, or the digits in the computer, are no more than the raw material of a process which includes the whole culture in which words and meanings are understood.

This larger story has to be told in its own terms if it is to be told at all, and our knowledge of ourselves at this larger human level is an indispensable part of what it means to be a conscious person. The digital code story, therefore, cannot replace the human story. Each belongs within its own context. The human story is in one sense the more fundamental, because the digital code, at least in a computer, is itself a human invention, a means of conveying information deliberately abstracted from our conscious awareness, in order to tell a story reducible to mathematical notation.

It is also unsatisfactory to claim, as Dennett does in referring to the brain, that only materialistic explanations will suffice. The concept of matter is itself an abstraction – admittedly an extremely useful, indeed necessary, one – from our conscious experience of what is other than ourselves. To explain away this conscious experience, or to deny it, is to substitute abstractions (such as numbers or particles of matter) for what we know by direct observation, and hence to cut away from under our feet the primary ground of all knowledge.

How the different stories relate to one another is, of course, a subject for investigation. That there is a need for them both is already perfectly well known to philosophers like Dennett, who in a later book, *Darwin's Dangerous Idea*, makes much of human uniqueness and proceeds to wax lyrical about what others would call a spiritual appreciation of the wonder and richness of human experience. How then does Dennett bridge the gulf between this quasi-religious acknowledgment of the significance of human life and his insistence that material reality is all there is? He writes at enormous length, with much subtle argumentation, and it would be ridiculous to try to summarise him here. If I understand him right, however, his crucial leap from using the language of hard-nosed, objective analysis to using the language of human consciousness relies on the concept of 'memes' invented by the zoologist Richard Dawkins, best known for his book, *The Selfish Gene*.

Memes, according to Dawkins, play the role in cultural evolution that genes play in biological evolution. They are the units of cultural heredity, which have the power to replicate themselves by fixing themselves in people's minds. Precisely what constitutes a meme is not entirely clear. They can be defined as the smallest identifiable cultural units 'that replicate themselves with reliability and fecundity' – ideas, inventions, concepts which stick around and go on being fruitful, forming part of the mental furniture of an increasing number of people. A typical list, according to Dennett, might include such concepts as 'wheel, wearing clothes, vendetta, calendar, the Odyssey' and even 'education'. Human consciousness, then, 'is itself a huge complex of memes (or more exactly meme-effects in brains)'. (p. 344). His idea seems to be that within the brain there is no single, definitive stream of consciousness, and no central point at which meaning is discerned or expressed, but rather a jumble of competing activities which are knocked into shape partly by 'the predesigned gifts of culture. Thousands of memes, mostly borne by language, but also by wordless "images" and other data structures, take up residence in an individual brain, shaping its tendencies and thereby turning it into a mind' (p. 365).

This is a complex set of ideas which would take me too far astray if I were to try to expound it more fully. I quote the passage to show the centrality of memes in Dennett's thought. In itself the idea of memes has an attraction. Concepts do evolve, do stick in the mind, are transmitted from one mind to another, and so become popular. But they are a job lot, difficult to fit into a coherent category with any precision, as the list above reveals, and there is a tendency for those who use the word to apply it to almost anything which takes their fancy. The meme for 'faith', we are solemnly assured, is an effective replicator because it discourages the exercise of the sort of critical judgment which might decide that it was not a good idea. This self-protective covering around faith, so the argument goes, can thus account for the persistence of religion in a world which at the present stage of history ought to know better.

This argument, if it can be called such, is a fair example of the kind of superficialities to which the concept of memes can lead. As anyone with any personal knowledge of faith will know, while it can indeed encourage some people to shut their eyes to uncomfortable facts, it can equally well give others the courage to explore the unknown. The opposite of faith *can* be doubt, but it can equally well be fear. In fact, even in a strictly religious setting, faith can have widely different meanings in different contexts and different cultures. Nor is it just a religious concept. Scientists themselves – including, or especially, the most critical of them – depend on a kind of faith in following their hunches and in believing that their efforts will eventually be rewarded. Concepts of this degree of generality are not discrete and fixed entities like genes. There is no 'essence of faith', or of any other member of the curious meme hotchpotch, which could be transmitted like a gene. The analogy with genetic evolution is therefore worthless. The whole theory of memes is no more than a pseudo-scientific description of how ideas move around.

There is worse to follow. Even if it is accepted that the theory is a useful one, it cannot act as a bridge between the world of brain activity and the world of human meaning, as Dennett wants it to, because memes already belong in the world of human meaning. Where else do concepts exist except in the minds of people, in their cultural artefacts, and as part of the human story? To try to insert them into the story of brain activity on the basis of a spurious analogy with genetics, and by pretending that they belong simply within the world of scientifically describable objects, is merely sleight of hand.

I have used Dennett as an illustration because on the whole I respect his erudition and enjoy the vigour of his writing, but it is clear to me, as to most of his fellow philosophers, that this kind of explanation of consciousness will not work. Even if better theories are devised, as no doubt they will be, it seems likely that consciousness itself will not prove to be the most significant aspect of being human which needs explanation. I have already slipped into referring instead to the world of human meaning, and it is this reality, the fact that our lives are bound up with such notions as significance, value and relationships, and awareness of being an agent, which takes us nearest to the heart of being a person – whatever story we decide to tell about the functioning of our brains.

Emergent properties

Implicit in Chapter 5 was the concept of emergence. At higher levels of complexity in a system, new properties can emerge which are different in kind from those at lower levels. An engine can do things, for example, which its component parts by themselves cannot. The difference lies in organised complexity, not just in adding parts, but adding them in significant relationship to one another. A book is much more than letters on a page, although at one level of analysis that is all it is. Unless I am wasting my time, the result of reading a book is to have received something on the level of personal experience. The same is true of the brain. Its complex structures can be dissected and analysed, and its evolutionary history can – at least in principle – be traced, but it cannot be understood without acknowledging the new properties which have emerged through its organised complexity. Furthermore, these mental properties are not based merely on the complexity of its structure, but derive also from the processes of its formation, from the interaction with other minds, and from successive exposure to a long series of cultural contents.

The organised complexity which makes us what we are, therefore, extends outside ourselves, in that each of us belongs within a larger system which has had a role in our formation. As I shall argue in Chapter 9, we have inherited mental traits from our evolutionary history and we need in part to understand ourselves as components of this evolutionary stream. Even more important are the numerous means by which the larger cultural system has had its effect on us, through everything from schools, books, art and conversation to language itself. All this has had to be conveyed through somebody or something stimulating our sense organs. In other words, there has been a two-way traffic, whereby emergent properties result from the complex operations of our brains, but these operations have themselves been shaped by the environment and culture inherited from the activities of the countless people before us.

Does this two-way traffic, which is obvious when we look at the larger cultural scene, have any counterpart when we turn to the question of how individual brains might function? If new mental properties can emerge from a complex brain, can these mental properties in turn affect the detailed operation of the physiological processes which support them? It would be strange if they did not, since one of the implications of an evolutionary approach is that properties evolve because they give their possessor an advantage; in other words, they actually do something. So what is the point of consciousness unless it makes a difference to what happens in individual brains?

It is a question which is frequently discussed nowadays under the heading 'top-down causation', a concept closely related to what was said in the previous chapter about webs and networks. Explanations of how and why things happen need not be confined, it was said there, to the description of simple chains of events, as when a vase is knocked over and broken. Most events have complex multiple causes. Why did I catch a cold? Because there was a virus about; because I had been overworking and was tired; because I travelled in a train full of people sneezing; because I had been living on a poor diet. There may be a hundred different causes, some of which will be of the kind 'a virus got into my body', and others of the kind 'I was run down'. In references to 'top-down causation' it is causes of the latter kind, the influence of the whole on the parts, which are in view.

To claim a role for top-down causation in the brain might seem to take us back to the world of spooky interferences so firmly rejected by Dennett and his fellow materialists. There is a difference. Whereas there are good reasons for rejecting Cartesian dualism, there are not nearly such compelling reasons for supposing that the parts of a system are unaffected by the whole to which they belong. Indeed, because the brain is such a plastic organ, constantly making new internal connections between nerve fibres, or reinforcing or inhibiting old ones, and because there is strong evidence that higher mental activities involve the brain as a whole rather than any particular part of it, it might be considered the example *par excellence* of the way in which emergent properties can affect the operation of the parts from which they have emerged. Consciousness, in other words, really does make a difference. It is a tapping into, an attending to, all that our human environment has given us, an opening out of the human organism towards new realms of possibility. Iris Murdoch, in her book, *The Sovereignty of Good*, made much of this capacity to attend as the basis of moral freedom. And it is not hard to see its relationship to imagination which, if we are to believe Coleridge, is the 'prime agent of all human perception' and 'a repetition in finite mind of the eternal act of creation'.

This is a controversial area in which much more work needs to be done, but I hope I have said enough, first to indicate the intimate connection between mind and brain, and second to show that we still need two kinds of language with which to describe them. There is the language of scientific analysis and the language of personal experience, frequently described grammatically in terms of third person and first person perspectives. In the next chapter I shall look more closely at the significance of language and its role in shaping both perspectives. Before embarking on that, I want to look at one further hypothesis which picks up on what I have said about the evolution of the human head and points forward to the evolution of language.

The birth of homo sapiens

Steven Mithen is an archaeologist who believes that he is better placed than most scientists to investigate the minds of our earliest ancestors, because only archaeologists have direct contact with the artefacts these ancestors actually produced. In his book *The Prehistory of the Mind* he draws on many other theories from disciplines such as child psychology, evolutionary psychology and anthropology, all of which interpret the past in the light of present behaviour. But when we ask what can actually be known about how these hominids and early humans behaved, and what kind of mental life they had, the only contemporary evidence lies in the remains they have left us. Archaeologists and palaeontologists have to depend on their bones, their axes and arrowheads, and a study of the places where they lived, to unearth such slender clues as there are.

Mithen starts by describing the now popular modular theories of the mind, which are used to interpret the kind of selective deprivation I have referred to earlier as resulting from brain injury or disease. The idea is that there are various sub-systems in the brain, corresponding to modules in the mind, whereby particular, specialised functions can be performed. It has been suggested that in autism, for example, the missing component is the ability to be aware of what other people are thinking – a failure of empathy, in other words. It is a failure which seriously obstructs the processes of personality formation. One researcher has coined the word 'mindblindness' to describe it. Everything else in the mind may be working as normal, sometimes better than normal, as in the extraordinary case of the autistic boy who has become famous for his ability to draw complicated buildings. As far as social behaviour is concerned, however, autism is crippling. Without an ability to sense other people's feelings, it is hard to relate to them in any but a purely formal and external way. A vital mental module has failed to develop.

Using the modular hypothesis, Mithen suggests that our evolutionary inheritance has given us a set of relatively fixed capacities, mental modules firmly established in our minds through our genetic inheritance and able to function without the need for conscious attention. There is our ability to handle objects, for example, or to recognise shapes and structures, or our sense of place, all of them important skills for hunter-gatherers. Basic skills of this kind may not have to be learnt. Think of a very young baby's reaction to the expression on its mother's face. The discovery of the significance of smiles and loving expressions is not a matter of trial and error; babies seem to know from the start what they mean and how to reciprocate. The most striking example is our capacity for language and the remarkable fact, already referred to, that children pick it up much more quickly and with much less actual exposure to language than would be possible if the whole learning experience had to start from John Locke's 'blank sheet' (see p. 94). This is not to say that untaught children inherit a specific ability to speak a particular language, as if Chinese children have Chinese brains which are different from French brains, but rather that the groundwork for language, the sense of what language is, seems to be an inherited module. If this modular idea seems strange, the experience of being able to do several things at once may offer a clue. We may perform some skill, on automatic pilot as it were, without being fully and continuously conscious of it. Drivers, for instance, are familiar with the experience of driving, talking and admiring the view simultaneously, with attention switching from one to the other as something out of the ordinary attracts it. It is as though different parts of the mind have taken over different functions and are operating semi-independently.

In what sense, then, is the mind one? Mithen makes the intriguing suggestion that the relatively sudden burst of human development which began between a hundred thousand and fifty thousand years ago took place when separate capacities of the primitive mind, which had evolved for different purposes, began to integrate. The evidence from artefacts suggests that up to that point there were early humans with considerable skills, but very little capacity to learn. Prior to the burst of creative energy which accompanied the arrival of the first anatomically modern humans, skills appear to have remained static for hundreds of thousands, even millions, of years.

Mithen hypothesises that language, which previously had been used only for social bonding as in chimpanzees, mainly through the noisy expression of emotions, began to invade other mental compartments. Thus over a long period of time it became possible not only to locate places, but also to describe their location, and so to make more informed decisions about hunting and tool-making. New uses of language made it possible to communicate about skills, and hence to criticise and refine them. In the long run it became possible to think about thinking itself, thus setting the scene for modern self-awareness. It was in this crucible of change, set bubbling by the enhanced uses of language, according to Mithen, that the integrated mind was born and with it eventually religion, art and science. The key to it was what he calls 'cognitive fluidity', the new-found ability of our mental processes to range over the whole gamut of experience and hold it together. The instrument of cognitive fluidity is meaningful speech.

It is an attractive thesis which has aroused considerable interest, but like all such reconstructions it builds impressively on very patchy foundations. The development of the human mind remains a mystery.

My aim in this chapter has been to give a flavour of some of the science which has been slowly edging towards greater understanding of this mystery. The amount of work being done on it is enormous, because this is *the* scientific challenge of the twenty-first century.

I shall be very surprised if whatever new theories gain acceptance fail to give a central place to our unique human capacity for communicating in words.

8

Words and thoughts

When the author of St John's Gospel wrote his opening sentence, 'In the beginning was the Word', he was expressing much more than he could at that time have realised. Even so, he was saying a great deal. The Greek word *logos* (here translated 'word') also means 'reason'. It was used to describe the underlying order, or rationality, believed by ancient Greek philosophers to govern the way things are. It is the word from which we derive our word 'logic' and the various '-ologies' (geology, biology, theology, etc.) which represent ordered knowledge about the earth, life, God, and so on. In later Greek thought there were those who conceived of it almost as an independent reality, in much the same way that Wisdom in later Jewish writings (particularly in the *Wisdom of Solomon*) is referred to as if she were a person. The word was thus ripe for expressing the belief that God, as the ordering reality underlying the cosmos, had been revealed in a human life: 'The Word was made flesh.'

That was not all. 'The Word of the Lord' plays a major role in the Old Testament as the controlling factor in history. St John's Gospel starts by echoing the opening words of Genesis, 'In the beginning . . .', which preface the claim that heaven and earth and everything in them were created by God's spoken command. Psalm 33 verse 6 picks up the same theme: 'By the word of the Lord were the heavens made.' The prophets constantly reiterate the phrase 'thus saith the Lord' as the basis of their authority, and so strong was the sense that words were powerful that, as in Greek thought, the Word of God could almost be regarded as having an independent existence. Thus Isaiah 55 verse 11, 'My word shall not return to me void', prepares the way for the opening words of the Epistle to the Hebrews, '. . . in this the final age [God] has spoken to us through his Son.'

Those who first read St John's Gospel thus had available to them a range of meanings which enabled them to interpret the life of Jesus, both in terms of a rational understanding of the cosmos and in terms of Jewish history. It is not surprising that the earliest systematic attempts to define the relationship between Jesus and God should have built on the concept of *logos*. It was not to last. After a brilliant initial career, the word was later abandoned as a technical theological term, since it seemed too tainted by its association with a complex system of philosophical speculation known as Gnosticism. This threatened to turn Christian faith into a form of esoteric knowledge accessible only to initiates, rather than a means of salvation for all, so theological attention turned, as we saw in Chapter 3 and 4, to more personally orientated language.

What was not so well appreciated at the time when the Gospel was written was the extent to which the formation of human personality itself depends on the acquisition of language. 'In the beginning was the Word' is also true of persons. As we shall see, it is not words themselves which shape us as persons, but the ordering of experience made possible by language, which lifts us beyond the level of instinct and habit. In pursuing the theme of 'man made in the image of God', the concept of *logos* can thus direct attention to those special qualities of being human associated with language and logic, words and thoughts.

It is highly improbable that the writer of St John's Gospel should have had this in mind. Nevertheless, one of the interesting properties of powerful symbols is to suggest new connections, which is why I have given this chapter a theological introduction. It picks up a theme running all the way through this book, namely that being a person is inherently bound up with our relationship with God. This is an affirmation I shall try to vindicate in Chapter 10, but in the meantime my aim has been to demonstrate, by looking at different facets of personal being, how theological issues are never far from our attempts at self-understanding.

The nature of language

Language is central to what we are. It is a narrower concept than communication. Animals, including human ones, communicate in a wide variety of ways:

gestures, facial expressions, clothes, colours, rude noises, habitats, body language, all communicate something to those who can read the signs. A wasp's yellow stripes say 'keep away', as does a tiger's growl, or bristling fur. Social animals, like the great apes, communicate with one another through sounds and gestures, to express emotion, to aid social bonding, or to warn of danger. But this is not language as human beings understand it, because it lacks the essential elements which distinguish language from all other forms of communication. Sign language among the deaf, on the other hand, *is* language because, although it may not use spoken or written words, it *does* possess these essential elements.

What are they? Steven Pinker specifies three in his book *The Language Instinct*:

1 The relationship between words and what they signify is arbitrary. A few words, 'cuckoo' for instance, bear a resemblance to what their object is or does, but the vast majority do not. There is nothing to associate 'robin' with a particular kind of bird beyond the mere fact that in English this is its chosen name. Words function representatively; their meaning is purely a matter of social convention. This representative character makes it possible to have words – and in sign language, signs – for things, qualities, actions, or abstract ideas which are not tied to immediate experience.

2 Language 'makes infinite use of finite media'. The average, well-educated adult is likely to have a vocabulary of some sixty thousand words. The

number of grammatical sentences which might be constructed from such a vocabulary is astronomical. Here, then, is an instrument of enormous power. Its extent is limited enough for its basic constituents to be committed to memory, but there is no limit to the number of things it can be used to say. Despite this, as we shall see later, its potentially infinite range does not necessarily mean that everything capable of being thought or felt can be expressed in words.

3 Language works, rather like the genetic code, by stringing together discrete bits into meaningful combinations. Words are composed of a limited number of sounds or letters arranged in different packages. These words can then be structured into sentences according to a subtle and flexible system of rules (grammar). It is this power to combine separate units, by relatively simple rules, in a potentially infinite number of ways, which makes each language such an exquisitely sensitive instrument for communication – easy to use and boundless in scope.

All languages have these characteristics, but there is evidence of an even more significant link between them. One of the most extraordinary, and still controversial, claims in the field of linguistics has been the so-called Universal Grammar which Noam Chomsky, its discoverer, asserts is common to the whole human race. Despite the obvious differences between languages, in both words and grammar, there is evidence that all of them possess a deep structure which underlies our human capacity to learn and understand them. This structure, it seems, must have evolved before our earliest ancestors spread to different parts of the world and is now innate. Its existence is held to be the main reason why human infants can grasp so quickly how to use this enormously complex instrument, without having to go through a lengthy and laborious process of trial and error. It is because they know by instinct what language is and how it is structured that they can recognise what is happening when people talk in their presence. Some parents go to great lengths to help their children to speak, but even children who are neglected manage reasonably well. Without being deliberately taught, quite small children can begin to understand the significance of structural indicators, such as variations in the order of words. Infants do not often confuse 'Mummy eat' with 'eat Mummy', yet the concept of word order is quite a sophisticated one. To have to discover, not just in this instance but in all instances, the difference that word order can make, could be a mammoth task. Clearly different children brought up in different language groups learn different words and the significance of different placings and constructions; but the sense of what language is about, and awareness of different functions such as subjects, objects and verbs, and the fact that their order makes a difference, appears to be universal.

The detailed content and proof of this remarkable claim are complex and beyond the scope of this book. I find myself convinced by it, however, and I accept the implication that there must be something in our genetic constitution which makes our use of language possible, and which to some extent short-circuits what would otherwise be the highly daunting process of learning to speak. The sad stories of children who for one reason or another have been deprived of the opportunity to hear people talking – or of using other means of communication such as sign language – during the crucial first six years of life show how hard it is to acquire language when the genetic instructions for learning it have passed their sell-by date. Nature does not waste energy by keeping capacities fresh and indefinitely available, which is perhaps why it is so much more difficult to learn additional languages as an adult than as a young child. Young children, on the other hand, seem to have no problem in picking up several languages simultaneously and keeping them distinct.

Chimpanzees do not possess these abilities, despite the claims made on their behalf by some researchers. Widely publicised evidence that highly trained chimpanzees can learn to use sign language and put together simple sentences now looks distinctly less convincing than it did at first. One reason is that researchers seem to have been over-enthusiastic in imputing meaning and intention to signs which chimpanzees in the wild might have been expected to use anyway. Another problem is how to distinguish comprehension from imitation. Chimpanzees are quite capable of mimicking human behaviour without understanding it. A third reason for caution against treating chimpanzees as if they were undeveloped humans is that human beings are not descended from chimpanzees anyway. We are, at most, very distant cousins whose lines of descent diverged many millions of years ago, and who merely share common, but entirely unknown, ancestors. There is therefore no good evolutionary reason to suppose that chimpanzees possess capacities which might enable them to be trained to communicate like human beings, and not much to be learnt about ourselves by trying to make them imitate us.

None of this alters the fact that human language must have evolved from primitive beginnings. In the previous chapter I briefly described Mithen's suggestion that what was originally a simple aid to social bonding might have spilt over, some hundred thousand or so years ago, to include other mental modules, and thus led to the explosion of skills so much in evidence in the archaeological remains around that period. It is now time to take this suggestion a little further.

Language and intelligence

The idea that language began as a means of social bonding is plausible for a number of reasons. It is of its very nature a social skill. Words are useless unless they can convey insight or information to somebody else, and because the meaning of words has to be a shared meaning, the process of language formation has to be shared too. Building on this need for sharing, Mary Midgley has suggested in her book *The Ethical Primate* a convincing reason for the parallel development of language and intelligence. A certain degree of intelligence is necessary in animals which socialise (as distinguished from highly organised social insects), because living and working together is only possible if there is some means of resolving conflicts of interest other than by brute force. The more complex the society, the more subtle are the adjustments required, and the greater the need for some agreed method of settling priorities. Thinking is a way of testing possible courses of action without actually carrying them out, and can thus aid survival. To be able to anticipate the consequences of thwarting a dominant male may be literally a life-saver. If it were possible to reach some compromise, that would be even better. But corporate thinking and shared decision-making require a fairly sophisticated means of communication. If this is to be used to test possibilities, rather than just express immediate feelings, it needs some means of representing realities which are not directly present. This is what words do. Thus representational language, so the suggestion goes, developed as a means of handling social relationships in communities which were becoming more enterprising and cooperative.

It is an idea which fits quite well into Mithen's more elaborate picture, according to which different mental modules had been operating in semi-independence (at least in the sense of not being able to transfer skills from one kind of activity to another) until language began to integrate them. Whether or not this is what actually happened, the link between language and intelligence (incidentally brought together in the two meanings of *logos*) seems to be well founded. Language is one of the major inventions of intelligence and intelligence itself needs language for its full development. This cannot be the whole story, though. The fact that some people's imagination is primarily visual implies that it is possible to think without words, and I have already made the point that not all thoughts can be expressed in words anyway. Experience also demonstrates that not all those who are intelligent are necessarily articulate, nor all those who are garrulous necessarily intelligent.

There is, nevertheless, an important sense in which language and intelligence serve to integrate an organism, both within itself and in relation to its social and material environment. It is through language that we learn to classify our experience, to encounter not just a succession of, say, individual 'dog' experiences, but to grasp the concept of 'dog' as applying to them all. Classification has given rise to endless philosophical problems, from Plato onwards, but without it life would literally be just 'one darned thing after another', a succession of unrelated images. Our ability through language to relate things to one another is the foundation of the belief that we inhabit an ordered universe, a cosmos rather than meaningless chaos, in which word and reason are linked. Language, with mathematics the other great expression of rationality, enables us to discern a rational order which, it is claimed, is itself prior to language and somehow 'given' in the way things are. Such, in truth, are the very title deeds of science. To explain something is to set out, whether through words or numbers, its connections with other aspects of experience in a coherent, rational order.

Does language distort?

Inevitably such a tidy way of viewing things is challenged, and increasingly so in today's postmodern culture. If language shapes and unifies our perception of the world, may it not also distort it? If, as I have indicated, words themselves are arbitrary, are we not imposing on experience structures and categories which owe more to our fallible capacities, or to our wishes, or to the accidents of history, than to what is actually there? There is a further twist to this argument in the current trend to interpret all such imposition in terms of the pursuit of power. The really committed sceptic talks about 'linguistic imperialism', the attempt to force people to see the world in a particular way by dictating the form of their language. Some feminists have had a good deal to say along these lines, as do those trying to preserve minority languages, which are rightly seen as irreplaceable expressions of particular cultures.

To pursue these criticisms in detail would take me too far from my main theme. There is a general answer, however, implicit in evolutionary theory. Religious believers who are worried about evolution often fail to recognise that it can be a powerful ally in combating ultra-sceptical arguments which seek to prove that all so-called knowledge is merely an arbitrary pattern, imposed on experience by the prevailing culture. An evolving creature which took such a claim seriously and lived by it would not last long in a world where only those well adapted to their environment survive. Evolution is a harsh teacher, and its main lesson is that our responses have to relate in some fairly consistent way to the world as it is. Of course, times change. Responses which were once appropriate may cease to be so, and some of our human troubles can be traced to the fact that we are no longer hunter-gatherers or members of close-knit tribes, though we have retained instincts appropriate to these. But to claim that languages are so culture-bound that they impose radically false understandings on what is being experienced goes too far. If this were true, it is highly improbable that we would be here. It is also highly improbable that any of us would have developed the critical faculties capable of exposing such false apprehensions. Radical scepticism about our ways of experiencing reality invariably turns out to be self-refuting because, if carried through consistently, it destroys its own basis.

I therefore stick to the common-sense thesis that, although language undoubtedly shapes and orders our experience and itself needs constant refinement, it nevertheless enables us to develop more or less reliable forms of knowledge. By virtue of its flexibility, and because human beings are adept at inventing new concepts representing new realms of experience, it also opens up infinite possibilities for exploring what is not immediately present. Mithen draws particular attention to the power of metaphor and analogy as tools in releasing the huge creative ability which eventually gave birth to art, religion and science. The story, I suspect, is much more complex than he allows, but he is surely right to see our distinctive human characteristics as connected with such distinctive uses of language, and it is to these that I now turn.

Language enables us to know ourselves, to tell our stories, to reflect on what we are. This self-reflexive ability, as it has been called, is the distinguishing mark of human consciousness. We are not only aware, but aware that we are aware, and so on through an infinite regress. In Chapter 3 I referred to St Augustine's meditations on the depths of this awareness and how for him it was a way of knowing God. 'Too late have I loved thee, O thou beauty of ancient days, yet ever new! too late have I loved thee! And behold, thou wert within, and I abroad, and there I searched for thee; deformed I, plunging amid those fair forms which thou hast made. Thou wert with me, but I was not with thee', (*Confessions*, X, para 38). Self-reflection leads to the depths of the self, and beyond it to the point where language fails.

Expressiveness

Such inner exploration through language is only part of the story, however. Language is never a private possession. The knowledge of ourselves which it makes possible is always knowledge in relation to other people. We know ourselves, even in the depths explored by Augustine, through the medium of a shared culture. Part of this knowledge depends on the conveying of information within a particular cultural context, about which I shall say more later. But part of it involves the active creation of culture by the constant redefinition and reorientation of the space within which experience is being shared.

If I say, 'This is a cricket bat,' I may simply be naming an object for somebody who has not been initiated into the mysteries of cricket language. But if I say, 'That was a good hit!' as the ball crosses the boundary, the chances are that I am not adding any information to what everybody else has seen and appreciated. I am using language not to convey information, but to create a rapport, to mark an area of shared experience, while at the same time expressing for myself the significance of what we have all just witnessed. It is from such things, rather than from cricket rule books, that a distinctive cricket culture is formed.

The expressive power of language, the ability to articulate what is going on inside us and between us, obviously relates back to what I was saying earlier about its social origins in the sharing of feelings. This may be one reason why learning to express oneself is so important in the process of person-building and why the awkward phases of growth, when personal identity is uncertain, often leave people tongue-tied. We get to know other people and learn to know ourselves by discovering how to express what we are, not solely through language, but at least in part through it. In our beginning is the word.

As I have already indicated, this creation of an identity through language is a twofold process. There is on the one hand the necessary business of labelling. On average children learn words at the rate of about ten a day, rather as if they were progressively filling in

an enormous jigsaw map of the environment in which
they live. Adults faced with a strange environment
likewise want to find their bearings by a system of
labelling. If, for example, we visit a strange town, those
of us who are meticulous about ordering our
experience will almost certainly want to look at a street
map and identify some of the main landmarks. But
there is also another more personal, yet implicitly
communal, activity which entails taking an attitude
towards what is experienced, commenting on it,
evaluating it, sharing it, being affected by it. The town
we are visiting may capture us by its beauty, move us
by its history, haunt us with memories, disgust us by
the prices of its goods. We build up a different,
evaluative kind of vocabulary, rooted as much in
feeling as in information. Finding words to express
this is just as much part of the business of making
sense of our experience as is the study of a map. The
same is true in the process of seeking to know ourselves; we use language for both kinds of purpose.

This may seem a trivial point, but it needs to be
made, if only to resist the powerful pressures in today's
world to think of the conveyance of information as the
main and proper role for language. The computer
culture adds to this pressure. Processing information is
what computers are good at, so the more we come to
depend on them, the more our horizons will tend to
be dominated by computable information. This does
not, of course, stop people feeling, hoping, evaluating
and trying to express themselves, but such expressions
of feeling (or whatever) are apt to be regarded as purely
individual, mere matters of private opinion, not part

of the real world of shared public knowledge.

The drug culture underlines the presumed gulf between the public world and private experience even more starkly. The use of drugs to enhance feelings and perceptions presupposes that these are being sought for their own sake, irrespective of the route by which the experience is gained. The fact that such experience is largely private fantasy is not regarded as a deficiency; indeed, one of the merits of drug-induced feelings is held to be their disjunction from ordinary life. What drugs offer is precisely the kind of heightened awareness which cannot be integrated into what are doubtless seen as the boring, workaday realities. They are an escape from, but not a corrective to, a supposed world in which unfeeling objectivity and the amassing of bloodless information seem to be all that matter.

I want to assert, in contrast, that the shared world in which we express what we are and feel and value is just as central to human life as the world of shared information, and that the two cannot in the end be separated without destroying our integrity as persons. Consider the search for knowledge itself. Why does it matter? What in fact does 'matter' mean in this context? Evolutionary theory might come to our help again, and suggest good reasons why it is important for our survival to have access to reliable information. As we have already seen, however, the gathering and communication of information is an inescapably communal activity, and therefore has to depend on good social relationships and the shared feelings which give strength to community life. Thus even at this most basic level, the connection between language as expressing feelings and values, and language as conveying information, can be seen as essential for human flourishing. It ought to follow that any attempt to restrict meaningful language to the mere communication of information should be acknowledged as some kind of aberration. Yet that is the direction in which some modern movements of thought have sought to lead us. Just how disastrous it can be to try to put language in this kind of straitjacket is revealed in the story of the attempt to reduce it to logic.

Logic and its limitations

The story begins in classical Greece as part of the pursuit of rationality, a theme already discussed in Chapter 5. One aspect of rationality was dialectic, the method of argument pioneered by Socrates, whose aim was to subject ideas to all possible criticisms in the belief that what survived such criticism was the best approximation to truth. This Socratic method was more or less abandoned at the start of the modern scientific era in the new eagerness to base knowledge on indubitable facts and to express it in clear and distinct concepts, as prescribed by Descartes.

The other aspect of rationality was logic, pioneered first by Aristotle and later by the Stoic philosophers, who set out rules for deducing true conclusions from given premises. The most obvious and familiar examples of Aristotelian logic are in the following form:

All dogs have tails.
Bonzo is a dog.
It follows that: Bonzo has a tail.

This may seem so obvious as not to be worth saying, but the deduction is as important for logic as the statement 'one plus one equals two' is for mathematics. It can also be set out in a quasi-mathematical form. We could, for instance, call dogs P, their tails Q, and Bonzo B, and restate the deduction as: 'All Ps have Q, B is a P, therefore B has Q.' The advantage of putting it this way is that it distinguishes the logical structure of the argument from its actual content. It is true of any P which possesses the property Q, no matter what P and Q are.

But, somebody might object, suppose that as a result of some sad accident, Bonzo had actually lost his tail. If that were the case, the major premise 'All dogs have tails' would be false, with the result that it would be impossible to deduce from it whether any particular dog has a tail or not. 'Most Ps have Q, and B is a P,' can yield no more than a probability that 'B has Q'. Philosophers therefore have to devise more complicated ways of dealing logically with this kind of contingency, and formal logic sets out a whole system of possible types of statement and what can be deduced from them. The details need not bother us here. The point I am concerned to stress is that in such a formal logical system the arguments are valid irrespective of what they actually apply to. In this, logic resembles mathematics. Two plus two equals four whether the numbers apply to apples, dogs or alien spaceships. In fact, the relationship with mathematics is even closer. When the propositions in a logical argument are replaced by symbols – the P, Q and B of my illustration – they can be manipulated according to strict rules as if they were a form of algebra.

Symbolic logic, as this method of handling logical reasoning is called, enables propositions which might have been expressed in words to be reduced to their bare essentials, to mere symbols which might signify anything, and thus to be manipulated into yielding deductions without any specific reference to the actual meaning of the propositions themselves. All that matters is the logical structure. The meaning can be put back later, when the symbols are translated back into statements about apples, dogs, or whatever.

This kind of symbolic manipulation has come to have a new importance in our own day, because it represents precisely what is going on inside a computer. The input to a computer, no matter what its actual content, is turned into a string of digits (in fact into a complex pattern of electrical pulses which are either on or off) and processed according to a series of preset rules, before being translated back into words or pictures. We need no reminders of the enormous versatility of this method of handling information and making deductions from it. The fact that it can all be done by translating highly complex information into something as simple, and as abstract, as a series of electrical pulses should cause no surprise. As was pointed out in the previous chapter, our own nervous systems operate on broadly the same principle, a series of on/off impulses, though at a much higher level of complexity and with a vastly more sophisticated system of connections. There need be nothing inherently restricting, therefore, in the use of this kind of code, since all our sensory knowledge depends on it. The shortcomings of humanly devised logic systems lie elsewhere – in their inability to handle the subtleties which are meat and drink to the human mind.

In the previous chapter I also described the difference between the physical processes going on in our brains and the meaning of what is being thought or done in terms of telling different stories. In this chapter we have arrived at a very similar contrast, which I am expressing in terms of the difference between the logical form of reasoning and its content. We have seen that, in strictly logical operations, what the symbols convey in terms of human meaning is irrelevant to their logical relationship. In most contexts, however, particularly in ordinary human conversation, it actually makes a difference that we are talking about dogs rather than about Ps. It is not just that we eventually have to translate back from the abstract symbol to its concrete meaning. I have in mind instances when it is impossible to know what the logical structure is, and hence impossible to make logical deductions, without paying attention to the meaning. Consider, for example, the following three sentences:

Susan saw the man in the park with the dog.
Susan saw the man in the park with the statue.
Susan saw the man in the park with the telescope.

They differ only by one word, yet the grammatical structure in each case is different. In reading them we become conscious of the appropriate structure for each almost immediately, but it would be extremely difficult to devise a logical rule which would allow a computer to distinguish between them, because the distinction rests on a great deal of accumulated experience relating to dogs, statues, telescopes and human behaviour, as well as to the uses of language. Sentences like this cannot be analysed logically without reference to their meaning, and meaning is precisely what is lost when they are abstracted from their human context. This is why even the cleverest computer can at times be incredibly stupid.

Ordinary language is full of these pitfalls. I like the notice, said to have been seen in a chemist's shop, which read: 'We dispense with accuracy.' Not that such difficulties have deterred philosophers and computer engineers from trying to reduce thinking to a purely logical operation and language to an unambiguous instrument for doing so. In the seventeenth century Thomas Hobbes expressed the view that 'when a man reasons, he does nothing else but conceive a sum total from addition of parcels, for reason ... is nothing but reckoning ...' In the twentieth century the philosophical tone was set in the middle decades by Ludwig Wittgenstein's claim to have analysed the structure of all that was knowable by his rigorous demonstration of how a purely logical language was supposed to work. It was based on the concept of 'atomic facts', by analogy with the atomic building blocks of the material world. The world was held to be the sum of such atomic facts and it was asserted that everything describable could be shown to be logically related to these building blocks. What could not be so described was not knowledge.

Fortunately the concept was soon seen to be unworkable. Words and facts are not discrete objects which remain unchanged regardless of their context. Nor did it prove possible to say precisely what an atomic fact was, or even give a convincing example of one. Wittgenstein eventually repudiated his thesis, but in the hands of enthusiasts it continued to do immense damage by seeming to suggest that whole realms of discourse, religion and ethics included, were devoid of any meaning because their language could not fit this tight description. Arthur Koestler once described it as 'one of the oddest episodes in the history of philosophy – a man setting out to circumcise logic and all but succeeding in castrating thought'.

Beyond language

To be fair to Wittgenstein one ought to add his own comment that his famous book *Tractatus Logico – Philosophicus* really consisted of two parts, one of which had not been written and which contained all that was important. Unwritten books are not easy to read, nor in this instance is the one which was actually written. This hinted at its companion volume in its famous last sentence: 'Whereof one cannot speak, thereof one must be silent.' The hint was felt to be dangerously mystical by Wittgenstein's fellow philosophers and was thus ignored. Even without mysticism, though, there is a valid general point in the recognition, through failure, that the things which matter most to us as human beings cannot in the end be captured within this kind of logical operation. Indeed, language itself fails, even the most expressive language, when trying to put into words the heights and depths of human experience. Gustave Flaubert, who certainly knew something about how to express himself, described human speech as 'like a cracked cauldron on which we knock out tunes for dancing bears, when we wish to conjure pity from the stars'.

It is possible to see a little more clearly into these deficiencies by returning to the question of context. Steven Pinker in his book *The Language Instinct* gives a nice example of how even a simple sentence like 'Mary had a little lamb' depends on what comes after it. He suggests three alternative ways in which the sentence might have continued: (1) 'with mint sauce'; (2) 'and the doctors were surprised'; (3) 'the tramp!' They provide us with three totally different meanings. In human communication words are not isolated counters in a game of logic. They take at least part of their meaning from their context and from the associations they have for those who use them, all of which makes it extremely difficult to reproduce the actual subtleties of speech in a purely logical form.

There is a less artificial example in Laurence Sterne's *The Life and Opinions of Tristram Shandy*. As readers soon discover, they have a hard time in discovering much about Tristram Shandy's life or his opinions, because the book rambles inconsequentially from one topic to another, starting a story but frequently not finishing it, as the author is distracted by yet another story which needs to be told before the first one can be understood. Some two hundred and fifty highly entertaining pages are filled in this way before Tristram Shandy is even born. What is the point of such a shambolic tale? It has been suggested that one of Stern's motives was to issue a caution about the new fashion for novels, in which the author could assume a godlike perspective and tell the whole story of a life with all the ends neatly tied. But does anybody, even an author, know what actually makes people tick, what is important to them and what has influenced them? There is no limit to the exploration of the context in which a life is lived. In Tristram Shandy everything connects with everything else, and what we think we know is often interrupted or contradicted by the half-remembered reminiscences of yet another character. The whole book, in other words, is a glorious demonstration of the impossibility of compressing a real human being within the confines of language – let alone logic.

Logic is only one meaning of *logos*, however. Language in its broader sense, despite its ultimate limitations, is nevertheless an essential element in our formation as persons. 'In the beginning was the Word.' Our ability to use language is partly a legacy from our evolutionary past, and partly learnt by each individual as the means of initiation into our culture and community. In the course of human history it has been refined into an instrument for rational thought. In parallel developments it has also been enriched with personal meaning as a unique vehicle for expression and an indispensable gateway to self-knowledge. It takes its meaning from its whole context and one can never be sure where the limits of that context lie. But it is also itself limited. As Wittgenstein's later writings showed, his enigmatic remarks about the book that was not written reflected his own intense awareness of a mystical dimension, which was incapable of being expressed except in a way of life – a life which he attempted to lead, to the extreme puzzlement of his Cambridge colleagues. Perhaps it is poets who are the most conscious of what it is not possible to say in words. That was certainly the case with T. S. Eliot.

So here I am, in the middle way, having had twenty
    years –
Twenty years largely wasted, the years of *l'entre deux
    guerres* –
Trying to learn to use words, and every attempt
Is a wholly new start, and a different kind of failure
Because one has only learnt to get the better of
    words
For the thing one no longer has to say, or the way in
    which
One is no longer disposed to say it ...
                    ('East Coker', *The Four Quartets*, 1940)

As persons we depend uniquely on language; it provides entrance to much of what is distinctively human and it forms the major content of consciousness, but *logos* also points beyond itself. The limits of our language are not the limits of our world.

9

Human animals

Human beings and domestic pets are the only creatures which run the risk of becoming fat. In a world where hunger is the everyday reality for billions of people, the risk affects no more than a wealthy minority. That it exists at all is a curious biological consequence of civilisation. The ability to over-eat if we want to, and to stuff our pets, is an outward sign of liberation from the sheer drudgery of keeping alive. This is one of the differences between human beings and every other living thing; we have created leisure.

Other animals work and rest; they may be active or passive; they may even play; but animal play, like some, (though not all) human play, is part of the deadly serious business of learning. They do not on the whole strive for or enjoy excess, whether excess time to do things quite unconnected with the problems of survival, or excess food for the mere pleasure of eating. Only human beings stand, at least partly, outside the struggle for existence; only human beings strive to exceed.

There are more profound ways in which human beings differ from other animals, just as there are better ways of using one's leisure than stuffing oneself with food. But perhaps for the moment fatness can act as a visible – sometimes too visible – reminder of that 'something more' which belongs to human life. As human beings we can pause, we can reflect, we can fill our minds and bodies with what we choose – not simply with what happens to come our way or is easily accessible. For this reason, how people fill their leisure is often more revealing than how they do their work. The pauses in life, the moments for reflection, disclose what we are when the pressure of circumstances is relaxed.

Something more

One of the strangest features of the creation story in the first chapter of Genesis is that at its climax everybody is told to take the day off – including God. No doubt there was a good didactic reason for thus highlighting the importance of the Sabbath, but at first sight it adds a slightly ridiculous coda to the story, with the supposition that God himself needed to rest. Or is some more subtle theological point being made? Its meaning seems to be that, as with human beings, there is something more to God than can be revealed entirely through his works. In a scenario where creation is envisaged as taking place in six days, there is an extra day, a day when, as it were, God is simply himself and which thus acts as a symbol of his transcendence. It represents his ultimate un-knowability, just as our own excess time, in a day set aside for worship, serves as a reminder that life is more than work and that human beings also have depths which cannot be fully plumbed. As Søren Kierkegaard wrote:

> What does it profit a man if he goes further and further and it must be said of him: he never stops going further; when it must also be said of him: there was nothing that made him pause? For pausing is not sluggish repose. Pausing is also movement. It is the inward movement of the heart. To pause is to deepen oneself in inwardness. But merely going further is to go straight in the direction of superficiality. (*Purity of Heart*, pp. 217–18)

It is a short step from Kierkegaard to recognising prayer as another distinctive human activity, further testimony to the need for 'something more'. For prayer is essentially about pausing and discovering new depths in the presence of God. It is a reaching into ourselves and a reaching out to God, not primarily in order to gain anything, but as a means of coming to terms with what we truly are.

I have already used Michel Foucault as an example in the secular sphere of this passion to surpass human limits, to break out of conventional reason and modes of life (see p. 110), but in his case it was not by pausing before God, but by what he called 'trans-gression'. Transgression seemed to him the appropriate response in a social context he interpreted as being dominated by power structures, which diminished and dehumanised those trapped in them. Many lesser people have taken up the same theme, including those for whom antisocial crime has become a way of asserting their identity. Foucault himself carried the principle of transgression into the extreme sadomasochistic practices that eventually led to his death from AIDS. Nietzsche talked the same kind of language, without actually putting it into practice. His description of man as 'the animal whose nature has not yet been fixed' implicitly acknowledged the notion of 'something more'. Indeed, much of his philosophy was about the need to transcend the ordinary self.

In their different ways, these and many other avant-garde thinkers witness to an open-endedness in human life, an inability to define precisely what being a person is. So do much art and literature, especially poetry. The South African author Alan Paton wrote a meditation for his son who had just been confirmed, and it included these words on the meaning of ritual:

These are the inarticulate gestures, the humble
    supplicating hands of the blind reached out,
This is the reaching out of children's hands for the
    wild bird, these are the hands reached out for
    water in the dry and barren land.
This is the searching in a forest for treasure, buried
    long since under a tree with branches,
This is the searching in the snowstorm for the long-

awaited letter, the lost white paper that has blown
away,
This is the savage seeking a tune from the harp, the
man raking the ashes for the charm in the burned-
down house.
This is man thrusting his head through the stars,
searching the void for the Incomprehensible and
Holy;
Keep it always for your reverence and earnestness.

(Theology, vol. LXI, p. 315)

It is possible to argue with Nietzsche about whether or
not human beings are the only animals 'whose nature
has not yet been fixed', but it can hardly be denied
that our species is afflicted by a kind of cosmic
restlessness which seems to be unique to us. In the
previous chapter I made much of the part played by
language in releasing us from immediacy, thereby
creating new possibilities of experiencing the world,
thinking about it, and transcending it. Some people
believe that this is enough to account for what is special
about us and is the basis for all the essential differences
between ourselves and other animals. Others, including myself, believe that there is more to be said
and that, in striving for this 'something more', we are
not just exhibiting our restlessness, but are actually
reaching out towards a spiritual reality.

Human distinctiveness

The more immediate question, though, is why in the end should we bother about trying to define our distinctiveness? In earlier centuries the need to stress our privileged status was felt to be crucial. The dignity and worth of human beings was believed to reside in the possession of a rational soul, whereas 'brute beasts', even if they were more than the machines Descartes stated them to be, had no such soul and hence no such dignity and worth. Thus people could, and did, and in some cases still do, treat animals as existing purely for their own use. The question of cruelty did not really arise. Sympathy with animal suffering was mere sentimentality. Any blurring of the line between animals and humans was regarded as a threat. Vaccination, for example, was at first opposed by some people on moral grounds, in the belief that the use of serum from cows would 'animalise' human beings. Similar fears have been expressed in our own day about the possible use of organs from pigs in transplant operations.

Keith Thomas, in his book *Man and the Natural World*, maps the changing sensibilities towards animals in the centuries between 1300 and 1800, and has many delightful illustrations of how our human superiority was justified. According to one early Stuart doctor:

Man is of a far different structure in his guts from ravenous creatures as dogs, wolves etc., who, minding only their belly, have guts descending almost straight down from their ventricle or stomach to the fundament: whereas in this noble microcosm man, there are in these intestinal parts many anfractuous circumvolutions, windings and turnings, whereby, longer retention of the food being procured, he might so much better attend upon sublime speculations, and profitable employments in Church and Commonwealth. (pp. 31–2)

Others, however, were beginning to ask pertinent questions about animal feelings. When in 1790 Blake wrote the lines, 'A Robin Redbreast in a cage/Puts all heaven in a rage,' he captured something of the changing public mood. Horrible cruelties continued, but there were also growing doubts as to whether the 'noble microcosm man' really was so noble, and whether the gulf between human beings and other animals was really as wide as had been supposed.

In the mid-nineteenth century the whole issue was put into the melting pot by Charles Darwin. Much of the moral and religious furore which surrounded the publication of *The Origin of Species* centred not so much on questions concerning creation, or the reliability of the Bible (which was in any case increasingly subject to historical criticism), as on the apparent threat to human distinctiveness. Even Darwin himself, writing in 1848 at a time when revolutions were breaking out all over Europe, feared the results of his own work. If man is only 'a better sort of brute', he asked himself, what happens to his spiritual dignity and moral accountability? Furthermore, if these noble characteristics were to be undermined by his theory, how could the fabric of society be maintained, given that social stability depends on the possession of precisely such qualities?

The unscientific nature of 'creation science'

Similar social and ethical worries sustain many present-day opponents of evolutionary theory. One of the leading creationists in the United States has claimed: 'Evolution is the root of atheism, of communism, nazism, behaviorism, racism, economic imperialism, militarism, libertinism, anarchism and all manner of anti-Christian systems of belief and practice.' Few others, even among creationists, would be quite so comprehensive in their condemnation, but it is instructive that a movement which claims to be soundly based on science – 'creation science' – should concentrate so heavily on the supposed moral implications of evolution. Indeed, given the tendentiousness of its so-called science, it is highly probable that moral, rather than purely scientific, concern is the main driving force.

So far in this book I have taken it for granted that evolutionary theory is broadly true. In fact, I have used it as a kind of guarantee that we are not hopelessly mistaken about the nature of reality. If we accept that our evolutionary history has forced us to respond more or less appropriately to the way things are, the fact that we have survived in a competitive world proves that we must have got some things right. I must now briefly justify this assumption and indicate why I believe 'creation science' does not deserve the name science, and hence why our relationship with other animals must be taken much more seriously.

Creationist opponents of evolution make much of the fact that it is 'only a theory'. Of course it is only a theory. The whole of science is only a network of theories, some better established than others, but some so fundamental to a whole branch of science that it would fall into complete disarray if its theoretical basis were to be abandoned. What the atomic theory is to chemistry, evolutionary theory is to biology. It provides the framework within which everything is understood; and it has attained that fundamental role because in practice it stimulates an unending series of fruitful questions, answers and insights across the whole biological field. This is not to say that it cannot be questioned, or that there is no room for further discoveries about how evolution actually works, or no willingness to revise the evolutionary histories of particular organisms. Like any good theory it is constantly being adapted, but the basic idea – that organisms vary, and that those best adapted to their environment are those most likely to parent the next generation – has proved astonishingly powerful as a means of making sense of the whole range of biological phenomena. The vindication of the theory lies in this continuing effectiveness.

'Creation science', by contrast, is unfruitful because, despite much ingenuity in rewriting the history of the universe, its overall effect is to bring enquiry to an end. If the answer to the question of why things are as they are is that God made them that way, there is really no more to be said. To put the point more formally, Christians have always claimed that God is the final cause of all existence; but if he is also invoked as the immediate cause of everything which may at present seem difficult to explain, science becomes impossible. Miracle takes its place. This may not worry those believers who see miracles everywhere, and who counter every rational objection with the statement that 'all things are possible with God', but it means that, whatever else creation science may claim to be, it is certainly not science. In practice, creationists scavenge around for supposed difficulties in orthodox evolutionary theory, generally misunderstand or misrepresent them, and parade them as evidence that the theory must be false. Clever presentation of highly technical issues makes their objections appear convincing to those who are not knowledgable in the field and who for other reasons may be uneasy about evolution. By playing on such fears, and by asserting that the Christian faith is untenable unless they are right, they have managed to persuade about half of all Americans that Darwinism is false, and are regrettably now beginning to make inroads in Britain. Sadly, they make the fundamental mistake of reading the book of Genesis as if it were meant to teach us science, rather than as a celebration of the created order seen in the light of God's saving power. They thus perpetuate the disastrous assumption that orthodox science and theology have to compete on the same ground and must therefore be implacable enemies.

Daniel Dennett in the United States and Richard Dawkins in Britain have mercilessly exploited this supposed conflict in seeking to discredit religion. Dennett, in his big book *Darwin's Dangerous Idea* (all his books seem to be over-sized), draws a sharp contrast between what he calls 'cranes' and 'skyhooks' as the possible engines of evolution. A crane lifts from the ground upwards and can be used in building larger cranes to lift still higher; as a building progresses, crane can be piled upon crane in patterns of ever increasing complexity. A skyhook is an imaginary fixture in the sky which pulls things up to itself. Evolution, he says, is by cranes not skyhooks. It is from the bottom upwards, not from the top downwards. It works on the basis of a simple rule of thumb which, because it acts cumulatively, can lead to developments that at first sight seem far too complex to have arisen by such a simple process. Nobody supposes that a useful eye, for example, could have evolved as the result of a few favourable mutations. But a single, light-sensitive cell might have given an advantage to its possessor in a world where all other living creatures were insensitive to light. Building on that foundation, more light-sensitive cells, more effective nervous connections, a focusing device and so on could each have established a further advantage against competitors which might themselves be becoming more adept at using the properties of light. This is the crane principle – one advance building on another, not with any particular purpose, nor going in any particular direction, but driven simply by the need to keep ahead in the race for survival.

Skyhooks, according to Dennett, are an illusion, a relic of creationism. Not only are they unnecessary, because cranes will do the job perfectly well, but the idea that evolution is being pulled towards some predetermined goal undermines Darwin's essential insight. Evolution goes the way it goes, because those organisms which by chance adapt best to their environment are the ones most likely to pass on their characteristics to the next generation. Time and time again, in explaining improbable adaptations, potential skyhooks have proved to be unnecessary.

Dennett presents this contrast as an example of the polarisation between a scientific and a religious view of creation, and the malign influence of creationism, as a mistaken image of what Christians actually need to believe, is evident all the way through his exposition. He does not dismiss all religion, though, and in a remarkable meditation on the wonders of the Tree of Life he acknowledges the glories of what religions at their best have tried to do, and of the moral order which humanity has created. His only stricture is that we should accept the fact that all these wonders have evolved and are not a response to any spiritual reality above or beyond us.

How does he know this? Is he doing anything more than assert his own belief on the basis of scientistic dogma? It seems to me perfectly possible to accept all that he says about cranes, to understand evolution scientifically in terms of the gradual building up of an enormous number of complex forms from imperceptible beginnings, while at the same time holding to the belief that this is not the only reality. If God is, as Christians claim, the ground of all existence, he undergirds the process of evolution as he undergirds all processes through the operation of natural laws. He is the basis of the reality within which evolution takes place, but he can only be known as such when there are those who respond to him. That implies the existence of conscious organisms capable of transcending the natural order, who have the capacity for 'something more'. This alternative story, deeply rooted in our understanding of ourselves, can make sense of the spiritual impulses Dennett wants to celebrate. Unfortunately, since what he polarises against the scientific story is creationism, posing as an alternative scientific explanation, both sides are the losers.

I shall return to these issues more fully in the next chapter. My present concern has been to indicate why there are no compelling religious reasons for denying that human beings are the products of evolution, and good scientific reasons for believing that we cannot fully understand ourselves without taking our animal ancestry into account.

Sociobiology

In the last thirty years there has been a spate of popular books, starting with Desmond Morris's *The Naked Ape*, which have purported to throw light on human behaviour from this evolutionary perspective. Much of the material is entertaining, even fascinating, but the game of tracing connections can easily become superficial. Thus, to take an example almost at random, Desmond Morris writes of a mother's comforting heartbeat rhythm, 'It is no accident that most folk music and dancing has a syncopated rhythm ... the sounds and movements take the performers back to the safe world of the womb. It is no accident that teenage music has been called "rock music" ...' That may have sounded fine in 1967, but the popular musical scene has moved on. Would he say the same of heavy metal music? It is a trivial example, but it illustrates the danger of linking some characteristic, presumed to be as old as mankind, with some ephemeral aspect of contemporary fashion.

As an example of a non-superficial connection, one could cite the development of parental care in many mammals and the relationship of this to sociability. Animals which have to spend a long time feeding and caring for their young gain an advantage from the protection afforded by a social group. In learning to socialise, the group has to find some way of dealing with problems which only arise within a social context. How, for instance, is it possible to control instinctive drives such as aggression and sexual rapacity, which might be advantageous to individuals, but which could destroy the group's social cohesion? There is no advantage in being a member of a group unless there are ways of distinguishing between acceptable and unacceptable behaviour. That, as we saw in the previous chapter, requires an effective and quite sophisticated means of communication, and is why the development of intelligence and language became such an essential part of this process of adapting to a more social way of life. It is important to draw a sharp distinction, however, between this kind of society – found mainly among mammals – and insect societies, which operate in quite different ways, have quite different evolutionary histories and are based, not on individual intelligence, but on a rigid differentiation of function.

'Sociobiology' was the name given by the American naturalist E.O. Wilson to the scientific study of biologically inherited forms of social behaviour. He himself is an insect man, a world authority on ants. He describes in his autobiography how in the 1960s his role as an evolutionary biologist was threatened by the rise of molecular biology, which seemed destined to take over his entire field, replacing the study of whole animals in their environment by the study of their genetic development. He therefore moved to the opposite extreme and initiated extensive research on animal populations and their behaviour. This in due course blossomed into a new branch of evolutionary theory, which sought to ground all aspects of social behaviour – including that of human beings – in instincts and predispositions developed as a result of Darwinian competition.

Human altruism at first seemed to pose special problems, for what competitive advantage could there be in seeking the advantage of others? Wilson was saved, however, by an ingenious theory of kin selection which managed to demonstrate that, even though an individual might not benefit from some act of self-sacrifice, a proportion of his or her genes might. If the self-sacrifice preserved the lives of close relatives, then more of the family genes might survive than if the sacrifice had not been made. In the long run, therefore, altruism (at least towards one's relatives) can pay off, and its evolutionary origin might thus be explained on essentially the same principle in human beings as in ants – much to the delight of Wilson himself. This may not seem a very inspiring basis for morality and it is hardly surprising that sociobiology, and especially its application to human behaviour, became the focus of intense controversy.

Part of the problem, as perceived by its critics, lay in the attempt to force something as complex and varied as human behaviour into the straitjacket of a single explanation in terms of an inherited pre-disposition to altruism, developed as a result of evolutionary competition. Another and more funda-mental objection lay in the fact that this whole approach turned normal perceptions upside down by making genes the central players in the drama of life, with their survival and transmission being in the end all that matters. Dawkins took this inversion even further with his concept of the 'selfish gene', and described a scenario in which the significance of living creatures, and all that they do, lies solely in their capacity for making more genes. Both represent extreme attempts to reduce the richness and complexity of life, as it is actually experienced, to its simplest and most impersonal constituents. Both discount the significance of the new properties which emerge at different levels of complexity, and which need to be understood in terms appropriate to that level. Explanations in terms of selfish genes (a phrase which itelf involves a confusion of levels) throw little light on what it means to be a person now, or on the whole complex field of human morality, or on why some things which are in no conceivable way advantageous to us or our relatives nevertheless matter to us.

Consider again the question of altruism, itself a curiously stilted term, not commonly used in the discussion of morality outside academic circles. Ordinary people love and hate, are generous or mean, selfish or unselfish. If they see a child in danger of being run over, their responses are not likely to be affected by whether they share any genes with it. Of course, there are many circumstances in which family does come first, but the emotions which predispose us to act as we do, though generated within the context of families, in most people rapidly become more inclusive. We do not have to imagine an altruism gene, or set of genes, to account for such emotional responses. It is enough to point out, as I have done earlier, the kind of attachments which are necessary within prolonged parenting. Love is not an evolutionary mystery; in its most basic form it is a biological necessity, whether we are genetically predisposed to it or whether we learn to value it and respond to it through the experience of being loved.

It seems likely that a large proportion of our human characteristics are indeed genetically based. If, as suggested, our ability to use language and grasp grammatical structures is inherited, the chances are that many less complicated aspects of human behaviour are inherited also. To that extent Wilson and his colleagues were right, despite a disastrous tendency to jump straight from the identification of a speculative biological connection to a full-blown explanation of some complex, culturally conditioned activity. Language is a case in point. The fact that there is a biological basis for it does not mean that the development of speech requires no other input, nor that the study of linguistics might eventually be absorbed into biology. The new properties and capacities which emerge at new levels of complexity require new concepts and new ways of handling them. In the same way, morality may have genetic roots, more probably in the biological demands of parenting than in the genetic mathematics of altruism, but this does not mean that moral issues can or should be settled by an appeal to biology, nor that ethics has somehow been exposed as merely another by-product of evolution in action.

Human nature

To know that some of our deepest impulses have their origins in our evolutionary history can actually be helpful. It means that there is such a thing as human nature – feelings, instincts and types of behaviour which are natural to us, and which have not been imposed on us by the constraints of our culture. This is worth knowing and does not contradict what I was saying earlier about the open-endedness of human nature, the 'something more' which drives us to transcend ourselves. Human nature provides the foundations on which the house of culture is built. The shape, structure, stability and beauty (or otherwise) of that house depends on human history, and on the insight and example of creative individuals. Thus cultures vary enormously, but one which bore no relation to its foundations in nature could not survive for long.

There are those who resist any idea of 'givenness' in human nature, not least on the wilder shores of postmodernism and other revolutionary movements. Communism had a particular dislike for it, since it threatened belief in the all-importance of social and economic conditioning. Latter-day disciples still intoxicated by Nietzsche assert that the goal of human life should be to act as totally free spirits, a state in which we make ourselves whatever we choose to be, because everything is mere appearance anyway, a flux of images without depth or stability. The so-called laws of human nature are dismissed as shackles imposed by the powerful on the weak, in whose interests the powerful claim to be acting. There is a bizarre illustration of such attitudes in some of the videos which nowadays accompany pop music. The rapid succession of lurching, meaningless and violent images is presumably meant to represent a vertiginous kind of freedom. It seems more likely, though, that the illusion of unlimited freedom and creativity merely hides the fact that nature is having its say without the normal constraints of reason. Foucault, who typified some of these attitudes, 'waged a kind of guerrilla war, in theory as well as in practice, against the imperative to tell the truth. The exemplary individual, he insisted, "is not the man who goes off to discover himself, his secrets, his hidden truth; he is the man who tries to invent himself", uninhibited by the constraints of conventional morality' (James Miller, *The Passion of Michael Foucault*, p. 358). Foucault's story nevertheless suggests that there may be hidden truths about what we are, which catch up on us whether we recognise them or not.

The alternative is to acknowledge what nature has given us and to discover our freedom in directing it to worthwhile ends. The ends themselves have to be discovered and argued about and cannot be assumed as given by nature, for the simple reason that our instinctive drives, needs and predispositions do not all point us in the same direction. Our 'hidden truth' is that we are divided within ourselves, that we have goals which are in conflict, and that our freedom lies, not in denying what we are, nor in defying what we are, but in finding ways to act as a unity despite our divergent interests. What is true of individuals is true also of our social groups and that is why qualities like empathy, understanding, and a willingness to listen and to suppress or redirect our desires are so important. Rational thinking has its part to play in this, as do discussion, the making of rules, and the creation of structures within which freedom can flourish. All these presuppose that there are natural characteristics which human beings share in common, among which are the capacity to build on nature, to transcend it without ignoring it, and to strive for that elusive 'something more'.

Christian thinkers have frequently explored these themes without using precisely this language. The doctrine of original sin, which causes such offence to enlightened secularists, has empirical roots in the very sense of dividedness I have been describing. The freedom to be an integrated self is not an automatic endowment, but is given to us in the process of being loved, a love which at the highest level Christians identify as God's grace. It is this grace which according to traditional theology 'perfects nature', and which is essential if natural law – the law of our God-given being – is to be a reliable moral guide.

In drawing these comparisons I am not claiming that the scientific and theological accounts are equivalent, only that there is a close connection between them. They are saying things about what we are as human beings which are compatible, though they have different aims and contexts. They are not compatible with all interpretations, however. Theology, for instance, must vigorously resist any interpretation of evolution which locates the ultimate significance of the process simply in the survival of genes. It is what genes produce, and the lives which flow from this, which are important. The fact that it is necessary to say something so obvious is a measure of how far the excitements of modern genetics have confused many people's sense of values.

Original sin

There is a further task for Christian theology in trying to make its teaching about original sin compatible with what is now known about human origins. It can no longer afford an interpretation which relies on belief in a historical Fall. If we take seriously our animal ancestry and the long, slow development towards homo sapiens, there is no credible way of defending the idea that, at a particular moment in time, human nature was radically altered for the worse and that this in some extraordinary way affected the rest of the created world.

It is not theologically necessary to believe any such thing. If we ask why it has ever seemed plausible to believe in some original human catastrophe, the answer must surely lie in the observed fact that all human beings are to some extent at odds with themselves, as well as with each other. We have motives which pull in opposite directions, desires which are in conflict, goals and interests which do not match. As far as we can tell, throughout most of human history there has been an awareness of some spiritual reality sustaining and confronting human existence, coupled with the sense that all is not well with this relationship.

There are thus ample empirical grounds for thinking that there is something wrong with human beings, which affects the whole human race. The Jews knew this, and called it the 'evil imagination', but they did not link it with the Adam and Eve story, nor did they suppose that the evil imagination took shape at any particular time. It was St Paul who made the link with Genesis chapter 3 while developing his comparison between the first Adam and the new Adam, Jesus Christ, in Romans chapter 5. His motive was to underscore the solidarity of the whole human race – united in sin through Adam's fall, and united in the salvation available through Christ. This is a comparison which has caused endless problems and, as I have already indicated, it is unnecessary. It is also of no help in solving one of the most intractable theological problems – how and why, if the world and humanity were created perfect, did things go so wrong?

There is an alternative, linked to the name of a second-century bishop, St Irenaeus, who based his thinking not on the idea of a fall from some primitive perfection, but on the idea of growth. The Adam story, according to Irenaeus, belonged to the childhood of the human race. There was never a primitive perfection, but within the world with its mixture of good and evil, human beings can choose the good and grow into maturity. Irenaeus did not get far in working out the implications of this way of thinking, but his approach has obvious resonances with the picture of human origins I have been describing, and has become increasingly attractive to modern theologians. If ours is a world in the making, a world in which freedom is to be possible, then the conflicts and confusions, and the immensely slow process of development, may be part of the necessary conditions. Seen from this perspective, the Adam and Eve story describes what happens to every adolescent as they discover the power of choice. You want to know good and evil? That is to take on adult responsibility – to be as gods. But there is a cost to it – exclusion from the paradise of innocence. How then can we be saved? Only by love, a love which allows people the freedom to get things wrong and is prepared to suffer the consequences.

My aim in this chapter has been to set the concept of being a person in an evolutionary context, and to underline the importance of taking our evolutionary heritage seriously. This does not entail a commitment to what has been called 'evolutionary optimism', the belief in inevitable progress, or any assumption that evolution by itself can provide an answer to human ills or a definitive account of what human beings are. But it does provide a starting point, a reminder that we possess a human nature which is not infinitely malleable, but contains a mixture of needs, instincts, desires and predispositions which cannot be ignored if we are to flourish as mature human beings. It is also characteristic of our humanness that we have the urge to transcend this starting point, a task which throughout history has usually been the preserve of religion. I have a favourite quotation from Pascal which, though it uses theological imagery I have suggested is misleading, wonderfully conveys the character of this urge to transcendence:

> The greatness of man is so evident, that it is even proved by his wretchedness. For what in animals is nature we call in man wretchedness; by which we recognise that, his nature being now like that of animals, he has fallen from a better nature which once was his. For who is unhappy at not being a king, except a deposed king? (Pensée 409)

Or perhaps one might add 'one destined for kingship'.

Pascal also has wise things to say about the balance between our animal and our human nature:

> Man is neither angel nor beast, and it is unfortunately the case that anyone trying to act the

angel acts the beast ... It is dangerous to explain too clearly to man how like he is to the animals without pointing out his greatness. It is also dangerous to make too much of his greatness without his vileness. It is still more dangerous to leave him in ignorance of both. Man must not be allowed to believe that he is equal either to animals or to angels, nor to be unaware of either, but he must know both. (Pensée 358)

Speciesism

Before turning more explicitly to theology in the next chapter, I must add a postscript on non-human animals, in the light of this estimate of our close kinship. They clearly differ in the degree to which they possess human-like attributes. Some, such as apes and possibly dolphins and even pigs, may well be not merely conscious but may also possess a rudimentary kind of self-consciousness. In fact, for reasons I have already given, it is to be expected that all mammals which socialise will tend to have more intelligence and greater communication skills than others, and therefore probably a higher degree of consciousness. So some of the traditional marks of human distinctiveness may have to be reconsidered. If self-awareness is held to be the only criterion for joining the human club, then it may become necessary to face the prospect of opening the club to new members. Whereas, if rationality is the criterion, we face equally awkward problems about the stage at which children ought to be admitted, as well as about the status of those with serious mental deficiency.

These are samples of the difficult issues raised by critics of what they call 'speciesism' – the automatic assumption that human beings occupy a privileged position in the scale of things. Accusations of speciesism are a familiar part of animal rights rhetoric, and the word certainly manages to focus attention on the fact that animals have lives and feelings of their own which ought to be respected. There also ought to be much more consideration shown towards animals which have highly developed social systems. Blanket accusations of speciesism, however, go too far in my view. There is something rather perverse about language which seems to imply no substantial moral distinction between humans and other animals. Anti-hunt protesters who hold up placards displaying the word 'Murderers' might be asked to indicate whether they are referring to hunters, hounds or foxes. When other animals start worrying about *their* speciesism, it will be time to think again.

We human beings have always used animals for our own purposes. Indeed, our success as a species has largely depended on doing so. Without our use of them there would be little agriculture, little food and little medicine. Now that we are less dependent, it is quite right that we should be much more respectful of their lives and feelings, particularly in seeking to avoid callous exploitation and cruelty. We also, however, need to be more honest with ourselves about the inherent contradictions in our attitudes towards them. Keith Thomas puts the point sharply:

Oliver Goldsmith wrote of his contemporaries that 'they pity and they eat the objects of their compassion.' The same might be said of the children of today who, nourished by a meat diet and protected by a medicine developed by animal experiments, nevertheless take toy animals to bed and lavish their affection on lambs and ponies. For adults, nature parks and conservation areas serve a function not unlike that which toy animals have for children; they are fantasies which enshrine the values by which society as a whole cannot afford to live. (*Man and the Natural World*, p. 301)

We can, however, afford to recognise that animals have their own interests which need to be taken seriously, but to treat them as morally equivalent to ourselves is to overlook that 'something more' which human beings seek, and which goes to the heart of what we know ourselves to be.

In God's image

When Tony Bland's parents sat by his bedside for hour after hour, day after day, over a period of three years, what did they believe they were doing? The fact that they fiercely resisted my suggestion to reduce their commitment is an indication that, whatever it was, it mattered to them. I have no privileged access to their thoughts, but their behaviour can certainly be interpreted in terms of faith, hope and love. They must have had some faith that, simply by being there, they could help their son's mind re-establish contact with his familiar world. The hope against hope that some recovery was possible must have kept them going through the long period of deepening despair. Giving substance to both faith and hope, there clearly was abiding love, a willingness to sacrifice much of their own lives and happiness for the sake of their son.

They would probably not have described their motives entirely in these terms, though I hope they would have recognised them. I have deliberately used religious language, because in extreme circumstances like this it is often only religious language which can carry the full weight of what is being experienced. It can help to locate human actions in a wider frame of reference and thus enlarge their meaning. This in turn can release new resources to deal with them. Faith can draw strength from reliance on God's own faithfulness; hope can rest on the 'surprisingness' of God, who brings life out of death; and love can be fed by the love of God which first called us into being. This is not to claim that such religiously interpreted faith, hope and love are any more sincere than one might find in good, non-religious parents – only that they have a broader base in beliefs about the way the world is, and in the tradition which has shaped many of our instinctive responses. In extreme situations this can make all the difference, and is no doubt why many people discover a new significance in religious faith when the safe confines of their own world have been breached.

Linguistic impoverishment

In previous chapters I have frequently referred to the human drive to transcend ourselves, to push beyond the boundaries of ordinary experience and language towards what cannot be fully described or comprehended. The most familiar way of stretching the boundaries of language is through the use of metaphor and analogy. Words can take wings, can feed the imagination, can be released from mere descriptiveness; they can be charged with meaning, drawing on the richness of multiple uses in other contexts. The word 'cross', for example, carries an enormous weight of association in the hymn line 'When I survey the wondrous Cross', which it entirely lacks in the context of a ballot paper. Poetry makes use of this flexibility of language, and it is often through the striking juxtaposition of different images, or the use of words in unusual contexts, that it generates insights which might be impossible to express in straightforward prose.

The most characteristic use of stretched and over-loaded language is in religion, where words usually have a long and complex history. Thus in Christian tradition the word 'faith' has no simple definition, but carries rich overtones from the whole of the Bible story. Indeed, one way of describing the Bible is as the record of a vast experiment in faith. Within it no word carries more weight, or is more difficult to define, than the word 'God'. Its meaning is in its use, naming the One towards whom human beings have aspired throughout the ages, with whom they have wrestled, to whom they have prayed, by whom they have been challenged and comforted, and in whom they have found peace and fulfilment.

Ever since the Bible began to become less familiar as a key element in our general culture, words which once were full of resonances have suffered an attenuation in meaning, with the result that it is now difficult to communicate about spiritual attitudes and feelings which may well be present, but cannot find an acceptable way of expressing themselves. A famous study of religious experience conducted in the 1980s identified this phenomenon. In-depth interviews with a large number of people in Nottingham revealed that well over half of those questioned had had experiences which were important to them and could properly be called spiritual. Yet the experiences had for the most part been suppressed by those who had no readily available language in which to describe them. Some people were afraid of looking foolish; some were simply puzzled; only a few were able to integrate the experience into their lives. Poverty of language, in other words, can entail poverty of experience, unless some other symbolism is invented which can carry sufficient weight.

The crowds with their flowers and other memorabilia at the Hillsborough and Anfield football grounds attempted to answer this need within their particular sub-culture by making an inarticulate, but profoundly moving, response to an overwhelming event. Being in the place itself alongside other people, and leaving there some token of their concern, allowed all sorts of mixed emotions to be expressed without having to identify these or put them into words. The Liverpool theme song 'You'll never walk alone' took on new meaning. The same kind of symbolism was revived, enormously magnified, in the public out-pouring of grief over the death of Princess Diana. There were the same crowds, the same flowers and other gifts, the same sense of shock at sudden and untimely death, and even the same identification with a song which captured the public mood. The traditional forms and language of mourning were not felt to be enough in either case, because they did not seem to carry the right resonances in a popular culture which no longer understands or values them. In the case of Princess Diana the traditional way of doing things also seemed to be too closely associated with the kind of formality and aloofness she herself had rejected. It is ironic that her highly personalised burial service, admirable and inevitable though it was in the circumstances, obscured the very message that the traditional service conveys so well, namely that all are equal in death – monarchs and paupers alike.

There are problems, therefore, for those who want to use traditional religious imagery to tap into profound human experience, and I have no doubt there are readers who have already been alienated by my use of such imagery at various points in previous chapters. My purpose has been to illustrate how the actual development of our self-understanding as persons in the Western world has, as a matter of historical fact, been intertwined with insights derived from Christian theology. Nevertheless, it is a connection which has been weakening. To stress its significance, as I shall in this chapter, may have the appearance of a Christian takeover bid for aspects of human personality which belong more widely to human beings as such. That is not my intention.

One of the great difficulties in trying to communicate Christian insights today lies in the – not entirely undeserved – public perception that advocates of the Christian faith are more concerned about winning recruits for particular styles of belief and conduct than with enlarging people's vision of what it is to be human. Yet what we are as human beings must surely take priority over the way we describe our commitments. A wise priest, R.E.C. Browne, writing about preaching, put the point this way: 'The Church says to everyone born, "Your vocation is to be human, and the way to be human is to be a Christian" ' (*The Ministry of the Word*, p. 69). He went on to describe the aim of preaching as 'wounding people with the revelation of their greatness . . . great preaching, like great poetry, deals with love and death, with life and birth, with hate and treachery in such a way that something significant is said about the tragic aspect of human life' (p. 80). There are echoes here of Pascal. The Christian faith is not so much a package to be sold, as an invitation to share an exploration of the human condition in the light of Christ. That is why it must have a continuing place in any discussion of what it means to be a person, but if the language is no longer understood, if the symbolism has faded, areas of meaning may become inaccessible. Many people today have been left with a nagging, low-grade awareness of something missing, a sense of spiritual emptiness which does not know its name and is in danger of being filled by an increasingly weird selection of do-it-yourself beliefs, divorced both from tradition and rationality.

Bringing a Christian dimension back into the discussion of personality, therefore, is not an exercise in surreptitious evangelism, but an attempt to recover an essential element of what human beings are. It is my aim in this chapter to try to justify this claim and to spell out some of its implications.

The personal as a basis for understanding

First let me face a major objection. In the previous chapter I dismissed creation science on the grounds that it would bring science to a halt by confusing belief in God as the ultimate ground of existence with the belief that all sorts of much more immediate phenomena can only be explained by God's direct intervention. Would not the same objection be valid against any attempt to bring a theological dimension into the discussion of personhood? It is one thing to say that ideas may have been formed in a theological matrix, but this does not mean that they still require that context in order to be useful today. Modern science itself was developed in an intellectual context shaped by the doctrine of creation, and in its beginnings depended quite explicitly on the belief that the universe was the product of a single rational will. But science has become self-perpetuating, and its faith that the world is intelligible is justified in the minds of scientists nowadays not by theology, but by its own successes. Might not the same be true of the study of persons? I have already given some idea of the number of disciplines, scientific and otherwise, which contribute to our self-understanding today. Why is there still a need to dig up old theological roots? And what are the grounds for thinking that the scientific picture is insufficient?

The various disciplines for studying human beings do indeed throw tremendous light on human life and personality. In their own terms they are as complete and comprehensive as all sciences claim to be, but none of them can capture the unique experience of being a person, because this can only be known from within. Human beings are not simply objects for study to be known in our fulness by external observation; we are also subjects who know ourselves directly from within, and our subjectivity entails an open-endedness which eludes complete description.

The usual way to express this elusiveness is in terms of the familiar distinction between a third person and a first person perspective. This is the rock on which all attempts to treat persons as if they were mere objects, capable of being totally described, eventually founder. Suppose this were not the case, and that it might in fact be possible to draw up a complete specification for a human being, to know everything about him or her. Then it would in principle also be possible to do the same for the person drawing up the specification, who would thus be able to have a complete knowledge of him- or herself. But this complete knowledge would in fact change the person's perception of themselves. It would become an added element in the data they would have to take into account when forming their theories and deciding on their actions. Furthermore, the understanding of the ways in which it would affect their theories and change their actions would itself become a further element in the data to be used in forming their theories and deciding their actions, and so on, ad infinitum. The point is that we run into the absurdity of an infinite regress if we try to produce some form of publicly accessible, objective account of all that is involved in our inside knowledge of being a person. It simply cannot be done. Descartes was right: there *is* a distinction between internal and external knowledge, even if it is not quite what he thought it was. There is something irreducible about our experience of being persons, something incapable of being caught even within the fullest possible objective description of that experience, and it shapes our awareness of what we perceive as being real. In the end our awareness always comes down to our own inner experience of personhood.

We can reach the same conclusion from a different direction by thinking about what is entailed in explaining something. To explain a phenomenon is to make it plain, obvious, transparent, not needing any further explanation. What is the criterion for being plain? At what point does explanation stop? Consider a fairly familiar concept like 'force'. The word is used in innumerable contexts – the force of gravity, physical strength, the armed forces, the compelling nature of an argument, the binding power of a law, a field of force, and the fundamental forces which hold together the constituents of matter. There is clearly a relationship between all these uses of the word, some of which are highly technical. In mechanics and physics it has had a chequered history with successive attempts to give it a precise mathematical meaning, or even to replace it altogether, as in the theory of relativity which reinterprets it in terms of the geometry of space. In many fringe sciences force is a favourite word; all sorts of things can be 'explained' by mysterious and hitherto unknown forces, whether from planets, crystals, or psychic healers. But what is it that has made this word so widely used, and how do we get a grip on the concept itself?

In explaining force to a child the obvious first step is to make the child push something, in other words to have direct personal experience of exercising a force. All other meanings derive from this simple beginning. This is not to say that when Isaac Newton defined force in terms of the rate of change of momentum, he was merely elaborating this simple picture. Clearly not. He was brilliantly creating a new concept. It could nevertheless link back into what every child soon discovers for itself, namely that the heavier the load you want to set in motion, the harder you have to push. Explanation has many levels, often including wonderful mathematical constructions, but the bottom level is direct personal experience.

The same is true in the world of everyday events. To explain the complex politics of Northern Ireland may entail numerous disciplines – geography, history, sociology, psychology, theology and so forth – all of which help to build up an objective picture of the situation in which people find themselves and are relevant to the way they think and feel. But why the members of different groups behave as they do will not really be plain to us until we can in some degree empathise with them. 'Yes,' we say, 'I might have done that if I had been in your shoes. I begin to understand.' As before, the bottom level of explanation is our own experience.

It may seem a large step to move from this kind of explanation to an interpretation of the universe in personal terms, but this, it seems, is how explanation began and why at first religion played such a large part in it. Most accounts of primitive religion underline the degree to which gods, spirits and personal presences pervaded the environment in which people lived and in relation to which they made sense of their lives. The history of religions can be seen as a series of immense struggles to refine, develop and rationalise these primary perceptions, and to discover within them more subtle and less immediate relationships with other levels of reality. Just as the concept of force floated free from its primary roots in experience and was defined in objective, increasingly abstract terms, so the primary consciousness of an all-pervasive reality in some mysterious sense like ourselves has been progressively detached from prevailing explanations of the universe, and relegated to a small corner labelled 'religion' – now dismissed by many as a mere relic from this primitive past.

It is customary to picture the universe nowadays as vast, remote from humanity and impersonal, while ignoring the fact that all our knowledge of it derives ultimately from personal perceptions. One consequence of this process of abstraction for many people has been to threaten their own sense of personal identity. It is hard to assert the significance of personhood in a universe which seems for the most part to be indifferent to it. Pascal, once again, got the balance right: 'Though the universe encompasses me, by thought I encompass the universe.'

I am not, of course, advocating a return to primitive religion, any more than I am advocating a return to Aristotelian conceptions of force. My purpose in this whirlwind tour is simply to draw attention to the way in which explanation depends on what we assume to be the bottom line, the point at which everything is plain. For some the bottom line is mathematics, but mathematics is itself a human invention, a technology, closely allied with, but not identical to, logic. And what is logic? In Chapter 8 we have already glimpsed some of the difficult and contentious issues which arise when logic is asked to handle matters of which it is inherently incapable. To believe that the bottom line of explanation must be in terms of some underlying personal reality does not jeopardise the integrity of other kinds of explanation at other levels. It in no way undermines or adulterates scientific explanations, which in fact derive much of their effectiveness from their rigid exclusion of the personal element – albeit at the cost of ignoring what is most directly known to us. Nevertheless, explanation which takes account of our own personal being can have a certain finality about it, which other explanations cannot, because the ultimate explanatory terms are derived from the kind of experience of which we are directly aware.

This is most obvious in our dealings with other persons. To understand another person's actions or feelings by empathy with them is to have a different kind of knowledge from that of the psychologist or sociologist, who necessarily work with general categories of explanation rather than from within a specific personal relationship. The different levels of understanding can reinforce one another, as when an expert throws light on a friend's behaviour which has hitherto seemed incomprehensible. Which most entitles us to say that we 'know' that other person however, psychological categorisation or personal insight? It has been said that we only truly know what we love.

Our understanding of the natural world has advanced hugely since the days when all events were ascribed directly to the will of God. But when we have teased out all the reactions and interactions, all the forces and particles and indescribable mathematical entities, there still remain questions about why it is like this. Why these forces? Why these apparently arbitrary mathematical constants in nature, which have been so crucial in making our world habitable? One of the more remarkable insights of cosmology in recent decades has highlighted the degree to which miniscule alterations in the basic properties of matter would have resulted in a universe in which any imaginable form of life would have been impossible. So why is it that the pattern of properties and forces came out just right? And how is it that our minds can grasp the amazing patterns which science has disclosed? To draw at this point on our own experience of creativity and choice is not to duck the further scientific questions. It provides a bottom line for making sense of the universe and of our ability to understand it, in terms of a transcendent personal will, with a finality which no further elaboration of mathematical equations is likely to supply. The only alternative at present on offer clutches at the desperate expedient of postulating an infinite number of universes, of which ours just happens to be the one in which life can flourish. As a scientific hypothesis that seems to me indefensibly extravagant.

It is the finality and irreducibility of this personal way of knowing, coupled with the open-endedness of persons themselves, which make theological insights so crucial to the understanding of what persons are and what a bottom-line explanation of the universe might look like. The subject matter of theology is precisely that which is final, irreducible, personal and, like our own experience of personal being, ultimately unfathomable. This is why it makes sense to stress, as I have done repeatedly in earlier chapters, how the knowledge of God and the knowledge of ourselves as persons have developed hand in hand.

The unity of the personal

The same conclusion is suggested by other lines of reasoning. I referred in Chapter 7 to Mithen's speculations about the sudden burst of mental development among our prehistoric ancestors (see pages 148–51). He identified the key factor in this massive change as a decisive step forward in the integration of the mind, a new unity between its different parts, made possible by an expanded role for language. What had begun as a means of social bonding, capable only of expressing social relationships, spread to include all mental activities, thus linking together perceptions, experiences and skills which had hitherto been concentrated in separate mental modules. With this new degree of mental integration the whole experienced world could potentially, if not actually, be recognised from then on as a cosmos with a unity of its own.

An important part of the linguistic development which made this integration possible was the growing use of signs and symbols to represent objects not immediately present, and it was this which gradually opened the way to an awareness of realities transcending ordinary experience. The concept of 'spirit', for example, seems to be extraordinarily widespread and appears in the most primitive as well as in the most developed religions. Interestingly it is often used ambivalently to refer both to human spirit and to divine spirit. The root meaning of the word, though, is 'breath', and it is the qualities of breath as life-giving, invisible, powerful, mobile, etc., which must have made it appropriate as a representation of the inner life of living things, a life breathed into them by God. From there it is but a short step to describing God himself as Spirit; indeed it becomes possible to conceive of a whole spirit world. According to this account, the concept of 'spirit' may have begun with the association between life and breathing, but it expanded in such a way as to throw light eventually on the intimate nature of God. The precise history is irrelevant. The significance of the story lies in the capacity of language to make connections. In the addition of more and more layers of meaning to words and images it becomes increasingly possible to develop the open-endedness, the freedom, the ability to think and dream and strive for what is not yet perceived and scarcely yet envisaged, which are now so characteristic of us as persons.

The other component, the new capacity for integration, likewise had enormous long-term implications.

To think of the cosmos as a unity, and to begin to relate this to the unity of the self, is a highly sophisticated achievement. One could write the story of modern science in those terms, given its foundation belief in the unity and uniformity of nature. At present great efforts are being put by theoretical physicists into the search for a 'Theory of Everything', by which is meant a mathematical theory bringing together in a single equation the relationship between the fundamental forces of nature. Whether these efforts will be successful remains to be seen, but they are a remarkable testimony to the strength of the belief among scientists that there must somehow be an ultimate unity in things, even if it proves frustratingly elusive. It is tempting to see this belief as a residual echo of monotheism.

I am not suggesting that anything like this sophisticated degree of integration was ever remotely in mind during our prehistoric human origins. There does, however, seem to be a kind of wholeness characteristic of the worlds in which relatively unsophisticated people live – or at least in those features of the world which impinge most directly on their consciousness. The immemorial fascination with astrology is hard to explain except in terms of a primitive gut feeling that human life and events in the heavens must somehow be related. Primitive thought seems to have been holistic to a degree which it is hard for moderns, living in our disintegrated culture, to appreciate. I am intrigued, for instance, by the persistence in much African tribal mythology of the belief that there was once a high god who made everything, but that he has gone away. The particularities of everyday life may submerge the consciousness of underlying unity, but it seems that a dim awareness of it can remain. It is plausible to suggest that this awareness of unity in the external world had its counterpart in the unity of the tribe, in the days before self-conscious individualism and the unity of the self began to take precedence.

The story could equally well be told by drawing on biblical accounts of the early history of Israel. There is the same dim awareness of primitive unity around a god who has been lost amid the welter of sectional interests in a tribal society; the same discovery that the unity of the tribe and the unity of its god are inseparable; and the same growth out of tribalism into a greater sense of selfhood and personal devotion. If it is true that a sense of cosmic unity and unity of the self go hand in hand, then the belief that we are made in the image of God can be defended as a valid theological interpretation of an empirical reality.

The all-embracing character of the personal

Yet another way of approaching this interaction between concepts of God and concepts of personhood is by returning to the point stressed in Chapter 6, that our personal formation depends on our relationship with other persons. We make each other. We discover ourselves over against the other. This mixture of being loved and differentiated, accepted and challenged, affirmed and corrected, not only gives us the basic tools for living, but provides the foundation for self-knowledge and self-esteem. But it can go terribly wrong. Relationships can be destructive as well as life-giving. They can offer confused and contradictory signals. They can destroy unity as well as create it, and for some the sense of being a fragmented personality is only too real. To think of ourselves entirely in terms of relationships can give rise to the modern fear that what we are as persons is simply the sum total of all those who have had an influence on us. Who or what are *we*, if we have been made by other people? We are back with Alice, fearful of existing only in the Red King's dream.

In practice the majority of people seem able to cope with an awareness of having been shaped as persons within a highly diverse set of relationships. Sociologists have developed the concept of the 'generalised other' as the sum total of all the actual encounters and influences which contribute to the formation of the individual self, and which provides the social unity over against which our personal unity is forged. But there is a still wider context in which this process can take place. If, as Christian tradition claims, God is the source and ground of all things, then he is the ultimate context in which all life is lived. What we are, and all that impinges on us, stand in an all-encompassing relationship with God. This includes our total environment, physical, mental, social, past, present and future, all of which exist in and are upheld by him, though not all of which, because of the reality of evil, point to him with equal clarity. God, in other words, is the most 'generalised other'. The sum of all our relationships and our ultimate identity are thus located in this ultimate reality. Our unity as persons, and the unity of creation, rest on the same ground: the unity of God.

Relating this to the theme of previous paragraphs, we can go on to say that our open-endedness as living organisms and our quest for self-transcendence as human beings, as well as our need for interaction as persons, are all in their different ways pointers to what we are – beings made for God and only finding fulfilment in God. Or to put it more simply and more religiously, I am what I am in the mind of God – the God who himself says, 'I AM THAT I AM'.

That is a concentrated and complex piece of theology, which I have put in summary form in order to show the structure of the argument. It is not in itself an argument for the existence of God, but for demonstrating connections between the idea of God and our self-understanding as persons. Arguments for the existence of God are beyond the scope of this book. For most Christians they depend to a large extent on the historical events which underlie the Bible stories. It is not necessary to accept all the stories at their face value in order to believe that they reveal profound and extraordinary truths. They represent an experiment in faith, the account of what happened to the people who lived by that faith, and of how it was vindicated in the life of Jesus Christ. To be a believing Christian is to identify with this tradition, not uncritically, but with enough confidence in it to make it one's guide for life. Other arguments of a more philosophical nature, some of which I have already touched on, can reinforce it, particularly in the attempt to demonstrate that the idea of God is not only credible but necessary. Important and valuable though such arguments may be, however, in the end Christianity is a faith, a communal structure of meaning, an enormously rich and complex tradition which holds in trust profound truths about human life, and which can only be tested by living in it.

Our identity in the mind of god

My more immediate concern is with the meaning of the statement that persons 'are what they are in the mind of God'. It is, of course, an analogy, as are all statements about God. The phrase 'mind of God' has recently gained currency in popular science as a description of the ultimate basis of natural laws. Why do the constituents of the universe, whatever they are, behave as they do unless somewhere, or in something, the laws of their being are imprinted? The word 'God' may be meant metaphorically by the scientists and philosophers who use it in this context, but the very fact that it is used illustrates the need to be able to refer to some reality which transcends the actual stuff of the universe to which the laws apply. The form of existence, as it were, has to precede existence itself.

Some cosmologists attempt to deny this in their highly sophisticated accounts of how something might have come out of nothing. There are well-popularised descriptions of how quantum fluctuations might have built up in some primordial vacuum and led to a separation between positive and negative particles, whose sum total remained nothing. Apart from the fact that a vacuum in which such fluctuations can occur is not, strictly speaking, nothing, there is also the problem that the laws under which this happened must somehow have been given in the nature of things – except that there were no things. At the very least the 'nothing', out of which everything is supposed to have come, must have had some properties which enabled it to become 'something', but the sense in which 'nothing' can have properties is not luminously clear. It is difficult to escape the implication that there must be something which transcends the observable world, and thus even at this highly abstract level, leaving aside for the moment its rich religious content, the concept of 'the mind of God' can be a useful one.

In that light it becomes less difficult to imagine how the form of a person might be held in being by God, even in the absence of all those physical concomitants which at present make up our existence. Computer technology has familiarised us with the idea that very complex realities can be reduced to bundles of information, which can then be stored in ways which bear no direct resemblance to the reality from which they were derived. On this analogy it is possible to imagine how all that is essential to our being ourselves might continue, even if everything except our relationship with God were to be taken away from us. The analogy can be misleading, however, for there is no need to think of ourselves as being reduced to bundles of information like some computer program, if we take seriously the view that what we are as persons has throughout life been consciously or unconsciously shaped by our relationship with God. If God is the source and ground of the entire context in which we live, then relationship with him must include all other relationships. What we are in relationship to him is held in his mind just as securely as every other aspect of existence. On this understanding, therefore, to exist in the mind of God is to have a form of being which is continuous with our present experience of being persons.

There are more familiar theological ways of expressing similar ideas. The Old Testament is full of pleas for individuals to be remembered by God. Psalm 106 verse 4 is fairly typical: 'Remember me, Lord, when you show favour to your people.' There is no hint here of remembrance beyond death, but a clear sense that being in the mind of God entailed some kind of security and blessing. In the New Testament remembrance points beyond death, as when the dying thief on the cross asks Jesus to remember him in his kingdom. In the account of the institution of the eucharist, remembrance means more than calling to mind what happened, but is seen as some kind of re-enactment, a re-presentation of its reality. There is an even more powerful metaphor in the frequent references to God knowing and being known by his people. Psalm 139 is a classic text: 'Lord you have searched me out and known me: you know when I sit or when I stand, you comprehend my thoughts long before ... Your eyes saw my limbs when they were yet imperfect: and in your book were all my members written' (vv. 1–2, 16). The prophet Jeremiah was acutely conscious of his intimate relationship with God. 'Lord, you know me, you see me . . . remember me . . . (12:3; 15:15). And there is a lovely image at the end of the otherwise rather wretched Psalm 17: 'When I awake and see you as you are, I shall be satisfied' (v. 15).

The belief that human beings find their identity and their fulfilment in intimate relationship with God is in fact as old as religion. Within Christian tradition it achieves its supreme expression in Jesus, in whom the concept of man in the image of God is finally fulfilled. This is spelt out explicitly in Paul's epistles, as in the reference in 2 Corinthians chapter 4 verse 4 to 'the gospel of the glory of Christ who is the image of God'. The degree of intimacy is conveyed in a remarkable saying in St Luke's Gospel: 'No one knows who the Son is but the Father, or who the Father is but the son.' (10: 22).

In the subsequent development of the Church, baptism became the main external sign and guarantee that believers do indeed share in this intimate relationship with God through their identification with Christ in the name of the Trinity. The giving of a new name and a new identity in baptism through a sacramental process of death and rebirth asserts, as clearly as any ritual can, that what we are in our fundamental being depends on God's initiative in making us, calling us, knowing us, sealing us with his own image, remembering us, and continuing to affirm us.

This, then, is the Christian answer to the problem of identity. Amid all the flux of changing relationships, different periods of life, developing and diminishing capacities, gains and losses, tragedies and triumphs, there is that which remains secure, held in the mind of God. The next chapter considers what it might mean when things go seriously wrong.

11

Diminishment

BBC Television broadcast a series of programmes in 1959 to mark the centenary of the publication of Darwin's *The Origin of Species*. The last of these was a discussion on its religious significance by a panel of distinguished scientists, plus a solitary junior clergyman – myself. Sir Julian Huxley, one of the participants especially renowned as a Darwinian supporter, was bubbling over with enthusiasm for a French book just about to be published in English, and for which he had written the introduction. His fellow panellists were sceptical. The book was Teilhard de Chardin's *The Phenomenon of Man*, a mystical, poetical, Christian interpretation of evolutionary history, which did indeed cause a sensation when it appeared and divided the hardline scientists from those who welcomed a broader-based philosophy.

In the course of the next few years I found myself reviewing at least ten books, either by Teilhard de Chardin or about him, with diminishing enthusiasm. Today he has few devotees. All his books were published posthumously and in consequence suffered from a lack of the criticism which might have enabled him to sharpen up his ideas, had he received it while he was still writing. Though a professional palaeontologist, he was also a Jesuit priest under the discipline of his Church, which regarded his interpretation of Christianity with some suspicion and forbade him to publish during his lifetime.

Evolutionary optimism

Huxley's enthusiasm for Teilhard was understandable. Both belonged to the 'onward and upward' school of evolutionary theory, which regarded evolutionary progress as inevitable and placed humanity at the top of the evolutionary tree. Huxley had written in 1955 about

> the primacy of personality ... [which] has been, in different ways, a *postulate* both of Christianity and of liberal democracy: but it is a *fact* of evolution. By whatever objective standard we choose to take, properly developed human personalities are the highest products of evolution; they have greater capacities and have reached a higher level of organization than any other parts of the world substance. (*Evolution in Action*, p. 144)

He claimed that 'in the light of evolutionary biology man can now see himself as the sole agent of further evolutionary advance on this planet, and one of the few possible instruments of progress in the universe at large. He finds himself in the unexpected position of business manager for the cosmic process of evolution' (p. 132).

Teilhard's vision, because it centred on God, was no less cosmic in its scope; he saw evolution groping its way, 'pervading everything so as to try everything, and trying everything so as to find everything', towards a defined end, the Omega point. This end was described by him as 'hyperpersonal', and was to be achieved by a rather alarmingly collectivist synthesis of all humanity, culminating in a summation of all human relationships in God. He described the aim of his philosophy in these words: 'To make room for thought in the world, I have needed to 'interiorise' matter [i.e. to ascribe some rudimentary mental properties to all of it] . . . to provide evolution with a direction, a line of advance and critical points [at which new properties emerge]; and finally to make all things double back upon *someone*' (*The Phenomenon of Man*, p. 290).

Such ideas are deeply unfashionable today. Modern writers on evolution emphasise repeatedly that it has no direction. The diagram of evolutionary change is more like a bush than a tree, with no main stem but a large number of equal branches, of which homo sapiens simply happens to be one. Such writers regularly point out that in terms of age, numbers, variety and survivability, insects and bacteria are much more successful than human beings; and even the dinosaurs had a very long innings, much longer than we can guarantee for ourselves. Who are we human beings, therefore, to assume for ourselves the kind of importance as the summit and leading edge of evolution which both Huxley and Teilhard ascribed to us?

Their language may have been extravagant; Teilhard's in particular frequently went over the top, but his phrase about 'making room for thought in the world' needs to be taken seriously. If I have succeeded in conveying anything in this book so far about our evolution as persons, I hope it is that human persons, products though we are of a seemingly blind process, have unique qualities and capacities; we are not only part of the process, but we can also understand it.

Given that our ability to think enables us to some extent to stand outside the process, to a degree which surpasses that of every other creature we know, we are right to regard ourselves as special and to treat our powers of thought as a primary clue to the nature of reality. It is not a question of pride or a desire to dominate. I see it as a necessary consequence of the fact that what we call 'the universe' is the universe as we *know* it. We have no access to the universe as it is in itself, whatever that might mean. Our thoughts are fundamental to what we are and to what we perceive. Furthermore, if it is true, as argued in the previous chapter, that we can only know ourselves in relation to a personal Other – whether human or divine – it is not so far from this perception of the importance of relatedness to Teilhard's belief that 'to make room for thought in the world' implies the reality of some ultimate, personal focal point for all existence. He has simply enlarged the scale, putting together the remarkable fact that we can think about the universe at all, and thereby gain a growing understanding of its nature, with the fact that this capacity is intimately bound up with our existence as persons in relationship.

Negativities

Nonetheless, 'onward and upward' is not an adequate description of what actually happens in evolution. The twentieth century has had to learn that there is no such thing as inevitable progress. Failures, tragedies and extinctions are as much a part of the story of life as the incredible diversity and complexity of the life forms which have flourished and survived. A Christian vision of the kind of world Teilhard was describing has to make room also for what he called 'diminishment' – the negativites of life, including death. Negativities are to be found at all levels of life, but Teilhard's clearest expression of what diminishment actually entails is to be found in a devotional book, *Le Milieu Divin*, which is possibly the best thing he wrote. Here he is on disease and death:

> Humanly speaking, the internal passivities of diminishment form the darkest element and the most despairingly useless years of our life. Some were waiting to pounce on us as we first awoke: natural failings, physical defects, intellectual or moral weakness, as a result of which the field of our activities, of our enjoyment, of our vision, has been pitilessly limited since birth. Others were lying in wait for us later on and appeared as

suddenly and brutally as an accident, or as stealthily as an illness. All of us one day or another will come to realise, if we have not already done so, that one or other of these sources of disintegration has lodged itself in the very heart of our lives. Sometimes it is the cells of the body that rebel or become diseased; at other times the very elements of our personality seem to be in conflict or to detach themselves from any sort of order. And then we impotently stand by and watch collapse, rebellion and inner tyranny, and no friendly influence can come to our help. And if by chance we escape, to a greater or lesser extent, the critical forms of these assaults from without which appear deep within us and irresistibly destroy the strength, the light and the love by which we live, there still remains that slow, essential deterioration which we cannot escape: old age little by little robbing us of ourselves and pushing us on towards the end. Time, which postpones possession, time which tears us away from enjoyment, time which condemns us all to death – what a formidable passivity is the passage of time ... Death is the sum and consummation of all our diminishments ... We must overcome death by finding God in it. (pp. 60–1)

The passage eventually turns into a prayer: '. . . in all those dark moments, O God, grant that I may understand that it is You (provided only my faith is strong enough) who are painfully parting the fibres of my being in order to penetrate to the very marrow of my substance and bear me away with Yourself.' (pp. 69–70)

This allowing God to undo us and remake us is the positive aspect of diminishment, the reason why in Christian belief it is a necessary part of every human life, if the self is to find its fulfilment in God. It is what is referred to in more conventional Christian language as 'taking up the cross'. But Teilhard is careful to emphasise that before we can lose ourselves in God we must first *be* something. His theology is not an invitation to passivity, but a recognition that to *have* to be passive, to *have* to face diminishment, can have a profound and life-giving significance. It is not to be sought for its own sake, however; a self-chosen cross may simply be an excuse for pride.

Although there are not many scientists who would today take him seriously, I have quoted at some length from Teilhard de Chardin, because he was surely right to believe that human beings need some grand vision of the cosmos by which to live, and which can make sense of both the heights and depths of experience. Scientific visions currently on offer tend to marginalise the very things which are most central and precious in ordinary human life, those most closely associated with our consciousness of being persons. Some accounts in effect leave no room for thought in the world and present a picture of a universe which is coldly indifferent to us. We are repeatedly reminded by advocates of such world views that we are insignificant creatures living in an obscure corner of the universe, and that we must not think too highly of ourselves. We are scolded for refusing to acknowledge that our real place is as denizens of some back street in a universal Slough, not, as John Betjeman put it, 'shining ones who dwell, safe in the Dorchester Hotel'. There is scarcely a mention of the remarkable fact that it is we, the insignificant creatures, who have discovered these so-called truths.

Others, less scientific, take great delight in the fashionable pursuit of deconstruction. Knowledge can be kicked from its pedestal by emphasising the relativity and partiality of all viewpoints, thus demonstrating by their incompatibility that no grand vision is possible. The universe has no centre and no meaning. We make of it what we will, and find its emptiness reflected in our own souls. It is the converse of my argument in the previous chapter. Without God there can be no unity, no ultimate reality, no vision, and the people perish.

The most familiar obstacles encountered by those who long for a warmer vision of what life is about, however, are not primarily intellectual, but are precisely the phenomena of diminishment which Teilhard was describing. It is not just that the stars seem remote and indifferent, or that the diversity of viewpoints overwhelms us, so that easy talk about 'onward and upward' takes on a somewhat fatuous appearance. The disincentives to faith lie much nearer home, in the daily awareness of tragedy, loss and failure. If a cosmic vision is to be believable it has to include some insight into how to make sense of these, not just on the grand scale of universal evolution, but in terms of individual lives. Indeed, a crucial test of the claim that persons are what they are in the mind of

God is whether it can throw any light on the various forms of personal diminishment, in particular the loss of those capacities which are distinctive of us as persons. There remain the still unanswered questions in the case of Tony Bland. How far can diminishment go before, in earthly terms, someone ceases to be a person?

Old memories

It may be helpful to start with a more familiar phenomenon – the gradual loss of capacities in old age. As the range of our physical competence is restricted, piece by piece, elderly people like myself tick off the things we know we shall never do again. Saying goodbye to them may bring sadness and frustration but, if we follow Teilhard, we might also interpret it as handing our capacities back to God, the calling in of a loan. To see our physical powers as lent to us can relieve the sharpness of loss. We are being reminded that it is time to concentrate on other things, what the old joke described as 'granny preparing for her finals'.

Memory is a more ambivalent capacity than physical prowess. The focus of memory tends to shift in old age, and it is usual to find old people more conscious of what they were than of what they are. The long-retired miner says, 'I am a miner,' because this is still the main reality of his life. The tendency to remember the distant past better than the immediate past no doubt has a neurological explanation, but it can acquire a more subtle significance than being seen as just another unfortunate complication in a brain beginning to wear out. Old people may bore the young with tales of yesterday, but the value of this for themselves lies in enhancing their perception of their life as a whole. A sense of life's continuity is affirmed when old memories, which might have been unheeded at a time when ambition and achievement were in full flow, regain their importance. A certain scepticism, born of experience, begins to question whether the new is quite so wonderful as it is made out to be. This is not to say that old people should be encouraged to be reactionary, or to witter on endlessly about the past, but it certainly concentrates the mind to realise that one has more past than future and, hopefully, more understanding of life than one had in one's youth. Diminishment, therefore, in a relatively untroubled old age, need not entail overall loss, but rather a shift in focus, as the first outlines of a different kind of life begin to be etched into the personality.

For some, however, the diminishing future holds only terrors. Simone de Beauvoir described life as like climbing a mountain. Throughout youth and middle age tremendous efforts are made to reach the top, but suddenly the realisation comes that one is going nowhere, apart from the grave. The summit has been reached only to find that it is the end of the path and there is nothing left to do but fall off the edge. Yeats described life as a long preparation for something that never happens. Interestingly, in the mystical tradition the same image of climbing a mountain recurs frequently, for example in St John of the Cross's

Ascent of Mount Carmel; but the conclusion is different.

What do you find at the top of a mountain? At one level of understanding – nothing. There is the same emptiness as experienced by the Roman General Pompey who, after his capture of Jerusalem, entered the Holy of Holies in the temple and found – nothing. Yet it was not mere emptiness. Any object present in the Holy of Holies would have diminished the awesome significance of the place itself, just as a restaurant on the summit of a mountain can destroy its magic. To reach the summit of a mountain is indeed to find nothing, but it is also to see everything. It is to view the world from a new perspective. To enter the Holy of Holies, conscious of what it means, is to be aware of God. To reach the end of a life might mean somehow being able to grasp the whole of it, past as well as present, to be aware of it as a huge vista, illuminated by the light of God's presence. Perhaps there is a preliminary glimmer of this vision of wholeness in the experience of those in imminent danger of death, who claim to have seen their whole life passing before their eyes.

I am speculating, which is perhaps all one can do on such a subject. If it is true, though, that the ultimate significance of my personhood is that I am what I am in the mind of God, then there is no reason to suppose that God's concern for me and knowledge of me is confined to a single stage or moment of life, or that the last moment has any supreme significance. What I am is grasped as a whole, a continuum in time, present as a whole in eternity.

There is an analogy with music which might be

usefully applied here. Music, like drama, is one of the temporal arts, but with a unique capacity to transcend language, much as a life transcends all descriptions of it. Musical notes can only be heard successively in time, but a musical composition is not an elaborate preparation for the final note. The final note may be important in marking the resolution of the tensions within the piece, and some pieces may end decisively with a final flourish, while others fade away into silence – just like death, in fact, which may be an event or a process. But the significance of the music lies in the whole of it, and in its power to convey what cannot be said. Nor does music disappear when it is not actually being played. Where is Beethoven's Fifth Symphony when no one is performing it? Perhaps that, too, is what it is in the mind of God. On a more mundane level it continues to exist in a variety of ways – on paper, and as recorded on tape or CD; in a rather less precise sense it continues in the corporate memory of a culture, and in the individual memories of those who love it.

Extension in time also plays an important part in poetry, as a means of 'thickening', adding density to, the experience of the present. T. S. Eliot, in making much use of historical resonances, was not just being nostalgic. The present moment by itself never contains enough to express its full meaning, which is why great poetry almost always has to draw on the resources of the past. In an age which discounts history, understanding is impoverished. If this is true of a poem, it is even more true of a life. The past, as it were, has to go on living in the present if the full significance of the present is to be known.

The idea that a life, as lived out in time, might be held in its entirety in the mind of God ought not to seem strange to generations who have been taught by Einstein to think of time as equivalent to a dimension of space. We have grown used to the startling concept that the deeper our telescopes look into space, the farther back we see in time. I use this as another analogy, not as an explanation, of the ultimately incomprehensible reality I am trying to feel my way towards. To envisage a life as spread out in time, held together on the human level by memory, but accessible in another dimension over its whole length, can give us a glimpse of what it is to be a whole person, known by God.

Personality change

It is against this background that we can begin to ask what might be happening in more tragic cases where memory fails, or personality undergoes some major change, or vital capacities are missing, or life has scarcely been lived. Alzheimer's disease is the spectre at the feast for the elderly. The gradual deterioration of memory may be alarming and frustrating for the person concerned, but is often even more distressing for those who observe it, and who watch the person they once knew and loved disintegrating before their eyes. The road may be a long one, and even in advanced Alzheimer's flickering signs of the old personality may remain. As it nears its end, however, the state finally reached is not unlike PVS, and the same urgent questions arise about how long attempts should be made to preserve a person who now lacks all visible signs of personal existence, apart from a still-breathing body. There are urgent spiritual questions, too, about what has become of the person who seems to have disappeared so completely.

Similar questions can arise in relation to those with advanced chronic schizophrenia, who exhibit total apathy, inertia, utter incoherent sentences to themselves and emit incongruous giggles or laughter while they sit in isolation from others. Nobody suggests that they should be allowed to die, but the person they once were seems inaccessible or non-existent.

Major personality changes, whether induced by disease, drugs, or accident, can cause enormous distress to those who have known and loved someone and now find them utterly different. The case of the man referred to in Chapter 7, who completely lost his memory but retained all his other faculties, poses hugely difficult questions about the continuity of personality. There are innumerable less dramatic, but nonetheless disturbing, examples illustrating the fragility of personal identity and its vulnerability to external influences.

Thus alongside the various kinds of diminishment as they affect individuals, there are the diminishments experienced by those who are close to them. 'Any man's death diminishes me,' wrote Donne, 'because I am involved in Mankind.' In the less elegant language I have been using earlier, relatedness is an essential element in being a person. Hence the loss of personal being entails loss for others, not just for the person concerned. That is one reason why those others are apt to cling so desperately to what they have known, even if all that remains is a mere shell. Though 'being in relation' is crucial to being a person, however, it is not the whole of it. Everybody has to learn how to survive the loss of relationships which may have been formative in their lives, and which remain deeply important. Just as in the passage quoted from Teilhard de Chardin the person suffering from diminishment can find God in it, so those who in varying degrees lose the person they love, or in other ways have to come to terms with personal tragedy, may discover depths in themselves which were hitherto unsuspected. There is something in us which cannot be exhaustively described in terms of the human relationships in which we stand. Beyond and including the human Other stands the transcendent Other, by whom our life is sustained.

Language about the soul is frequently helpful to people in such circumstances, because it feels more concrete than talk about 'otherness' and 'relatedness'. It makes sense to speak of somebody discovering their soul, or of the soul as maturing, or being obscured, or passing on. Belief in the soul can also be a source of strength to those who watch a person they love disappearing in a cloud of lost memories, or behind an unfamiliar personality. To know that something continues despite the devastating changes can make these more bearable, even when they are beginning to happen to oneself. I fully endorse what such language is trying to express. The difficulty about it, as I have mentioned earlier, is that it seems to imply the existence of some shadowy thing, 'the real me', which is undetectable and apparently unaffected by the body it inhabits. I believe the notion that we are what we are in the mind of God, and the notion that he stands in an all-encompassing relationship to the whole of our lives, can do the same work as the concept of the soul, but without running into the same difficulties. This is why I prefer it, despite its unfamiliar appearance.

Life after death

Diminishment strikes at the real me. As in a piece of music which fades out or ends in discord, the end is part of the whole, but only part, and by no means necessarily the most significant part; and it is the *whole* life which is held in being by God. We watch and mourn the processes of decline, the tragic losses of function, the empty shell of a still-living body, the sudden ends, but none of this need devalue or destroy what has been, which now belongs eternally within the love of God and henceforth will be known in and through the presence of God. What such language points to we can only vaguely surmise, but there are hints of it in descriptions of mystical union with God as known by the saints. There are also the much more widespread experiences of those who in some special moment glimpse the whole created world as imbued with deep significance, and who may subsequently interpret this as God somehow being discerned as the presence within it.

The justification for such language lies in the great religious traditions, and in the experience of countless people who have lived by them. To try to go beyond such experience and search for empirical evidence of life after death is in my view mistaken. It presupposes that the object of the search is some eternal core of personhood which can, as it were, be inspected and validated apart from belief in God. The many remarkable accounts of near-death experiences might seem to provide convincing evidence, given their frequency and their consistency, and there is no doubt that such experiences have been life-changing for those who have undergone them. Sceptical interpretations are possible, however, and it seems prudent to set these accounts alongside other claims to religious experience, all of which need the validating framework of a religious tradition if any sense is to be made of them.

Within Judaism and Christianity, belief in life after death grew out of belief in the faithfulness of God, a conviction that the God who had shown his trust-worthiness in rescuing his people did not create simply in order to destroy, or love and then annihilate the objects of his love. The climactic events in biblical history, which sustained this conviction, were experiences of deliverance from slavery, exile and other disasters, at times when hope seemed futile. The Christian faith built on this tradition, its central assertion being that God's faithfulness had been finally vindicated, and death finally defeated, by the resurrection of Christ. However mysterious and inexplicable this might seem to modern minds, something remarkable undoubtedly turned a defeated movement into a joyously confident one. To the first disciples the resurrection was the crucial demonstration that the Jesus whom they had followed had indeed revealed the true nature of God. It was seen as overwhelming confirmation of the belief that the God whose name and nature is love does not abandon his people in death. But it also makes clear that the life beyond death presupposed by God's faithfulness does not depend on the existence of some eternal spark or substance in human beings. The language used hinges totally on the concept of resurrection, not that of survival. Life after death, in Christian thought, is about the grace of God in holding us and raising us, not because of anything in ourselves, but through his own sheer love and goodness. The claim that he holds and values the whole of each life is a simple and obvious extension of this belief. This, in an absurdly abbreviated form, is the rationale for finding in the Christian tradition a reliable guide for coming to terms with diminishment.

What about those who have scarcely lived, those who die young, untimely births, aborted fetuses and, perhaps saddest of all, those who have had their chances in life and never used them?

The last category would really need another book, because it raises the huge issue of salvation. What is the significance of a wasted life? or an evil one? and how is it possible to redeem the past? There is a division among Christians between those who believe that life on earth determines what we are for all eternity, and those who believe that change and development is possible in the life to come. The former rightly emphasise the seriousness of the choices which have to be made here and now. If this life is not the arena in which our destiny is fixed, but might somehow be relived differently after death, what was God's purpose in creating it, or Christ's purpose in dying for sinners? The latter stress the incompleteness of life on earth, the unworthiness of even the best of us, and the unfairness of some never having had a proper chance. From this viewpoint the idea of further choices, as expressed in the doctrine of purgatory, allows time and space for people to grow into that fullness for which they were made.

Both sets of beliefs can be illuminated by the concept of God holding in mind the whole of each life. Life on earth, as it were, sets the parameters. This is the life God holds in mind. It may be long or short, but it is what it is because, in order to develop in freedom, it needed that element of distancing from God's immediate presence which the created world, in its distinctness from God, has made possible. True love has to allow the beloved space to escape from it. To imagine that similar, freely chosen development might continue in an alternative spiritual world would be to undermine this principle. Whatever is meant by the life to come, it does not make much sense, therefore, to think of it simply as an extension of this one. On this understanding, those who claim that this life is determinative of the life to come must surely be right.

Granted that the parameters of an individual life are set within created existence, however, it may still be possible for the significance and orientation of that life to be changed as it is exposed more fully to the burning light of God's presence. Such exposure can be heaven for those who embrace it, hell for those who reject it, and purgatory for those in process of facing the uncomfortable truths about themselves which the light reveals. Thus earthly life may in a true sense be determinative, without precluding the possibility that its fuller significance may only become apparent as the veils of self-delusion are torn away. To that extent, those who claim that there must in some sense be a purgatory are surely just as right as those who stress the crucial importance of life-changing decisions made on earth. Eternity is not simply an extension of time. Our life line is constructed in time, but new light may be shed on it in eternity.

I find it interesting that Nietzsche, having declared that God is dead, still thought it necessary to have some way of representing eternity so that his supreme expression of the will to power, his life-affirming, god-slaying superman, did not just have to go the way of all flesh and end in nothingness. Hence he arrived at the concept of 'eternal recurrence', by which he seems to have meant the endless repetition of all that was and is, with superman 'insatiably calling out "encore" not only to himself but to the whole piece and play, and not only to a play but fundamentally to him who needs precisely this play – and who makes it necessary: because he needs himself again and again – and makes himself necessary'. (*Beyond Good and Evil,* para. 56)

There is a rather sad little foonote to this theme in the recently reported setting up of an organisation called Afterlife. This is pledged, for a small fee, to take care of an individual's website on the Internet after the owner's death. A person's website, says the founder of the organisation, 'is a reflection of who they are, and what they want to share with the world'. There is a kind of immortality, in fact, in eternal electrical recurrence.

Nietzsche accurately saw that in the absence of God all that remains is the self. In Christian terms this endless absorption in self is an apt description of hell. It is on a par with the famous definition by Sartre that 'Hell is other people'. Between them Nietzsche and Sartre set out the antithesis of the belief that true personhood is inseparable from relationship with God and with each other.

Life before birth

I must now leave these theological speculations on diminished lives, those diminished by disease and death, and those diminished by their own choices in life, and return to the question of lives which have never developed to the point at which choices could be made – the stillborn, aborted fetuses, infants born without brains, or with other terrible, life-threatening deformities. Of them we can say in each case that what was intended was a human life, and that the bearers of this potentiality are therefore to be respected, even though the potentiality could never be realised. But can we say more?

It is in cases like these that traditional language

about the soul runs into even more intolerable difficulties than those I have already described. If the soul as a complete entity is present from conception onwards, given the high rate of early miscarriages, it would seem that the majority of souls in existence must belong to bodies which have never developed, never even achieved birth, let alone lived to maturity. In the economy of heaven this must create an extra-ordinary situation and throw doubt on the value of being born at all, if the unborn and those who have been incapable of developing any kind of personal life on earth make up the greater part of its inhabitants. The idea of a complete spiritual entity being created by God for each individual at a moment in time makes no more sense than the idea of a sudden transition from prehumans to humans in the emergence of the human race. Things happen gradually, and time is a dimension of our very being.

The alternative language I have been using, whereby the identity of a person is held in the mind of God, and the parameters of that identity are set by life on earth, can make better theological sense of tragic cases whose time on earth is minimal. According to this way of understanding personhood, an aborted fetus remains an aborted fetus. It has no further life except in terms of what it was, and what it might have been in the minds of those who conceived and bore it. It remains part of the totality of things in the mind of God, just as it remains indelibly part of the lives of those responsible for it – a consideration which might weigh heavily with those who make the decision to abort. But the meaning of its brief existence may change, both in the lives of others and beyond them, if God's love for all his creation, and his bearing of its pains and distresses, is accepted as giving a new value to what would otherwise be tragic incompleteness. This is the Christian hope of redemption, the gathering up of life's waste in all its forms.

As I have repeatedly emphasised, personhood develops slowly; there has to be a minimum physiological basis before even the rudiments of personhood can be said to exist. Thus an early embryo, lacking a central nervous system, is not in any recognisable sense a person. Nevertheless, the lack of personal attributes does not imply that such an embryo is of no significance. It is significant to its parents and to God, but not so significant that its potential to become a person should override all other considerations. At the earliest stage of all, when it lacks even the minimum of a clear physical identity, there seems to me a defensible case for not ascribing any degree of personhood to it, and thus allowing it to be used in research for the benefit of others. During these first fourteen days or so, there is as yet no distinction between those cells which are going to become the embryo, and those which are going to become the placenta. Nature itself is careless of embryos at this very earliest stage, before implantation in the uterus, and a high proportion of them do not survive.

The permanence of relationships

Abortion at any later stage is always a serious business and, as I have argued in Chapter 2, the reasons which might justify it need to be weightier the further the pregnancy has progressed (see page 27). The criteria I used in that chapter centred on the nature of the developing fetus itself, and its growth into personhood through various physiological indicators, culminating in the potential to continue an independent life outside the womb. In the present context my concern is with a different set of factors, with the significance of this potential life in its relationship to its parents and to God. The key concept, from this perspective, is that events and relationships are what they are. They may be ignored or forgotten, and their significance may be changed, but they cannot be erased – hence the dimension of seriousness in choices about the life or death of an unborn child. Once a relationship has started – and this can only be known once the embryo is implanted in the uterus, and more obviously when the presence of the child is actually felt – both parents have a responsibility which remains inescapably part of their lives, whatever they decide to do about it.

The givenness of such an enduring relationship can also be grounds for comfort in the case of stillborn infants. The pain of loss does not have to be shrugged off, but – like other diminishments – may by God's grace be woven creatively into whatever lies ahead, given the belief that even this little bit of life has its own abiding significance. Serious cases of deformity represent diminishment in one of its most distressing and uncompromising forms, the tragedy being that life will be diminished whether such a child lives or dies. Yet the amazing love and commitment evoked in some parents, who devote their own lives to someone who has scarcely any life at all, are a witness to the truth that even the most damaged personalities are precious. Tony Bland's parents come to mind again. They were, I suspect quite unconsciously, representing in their own family context the image of the God who does not let us go.

Yet the fact that in the end it was they who asked for their son's life to be terminated illustrates the awful ambivalence of PVS. It is a state between death and life, in which the outward signs of life seem to be deceitful, in that they carry with them no possibilities of a reciprocal relationship. Uncertainties about the diagnosis of PVS add to the difficulties, as do uncertainties about the conditions in which any residual consciousness might remain. No doubt more will eventually be discovered about the functions of different parts of the brain, and some of these uncertainties will be removed. But it is hard to see what a definitive answer would be like, given that the actual experience of being a person, in however attenuated a form, is not accessible to external observation. Apart from this direct awareness in ourselves, the closest we can come to an internal knowledge of persons is through our relationship with them. This is why the testimony of those who love and care for people in such desperate conditions must be crucial in the assessment of when personal life has, as far as it is possible to judge, come to an end. For three years,

Tony Bland's parents were, so to speak, holding his personality in trust. They eventually came to realise that nothing more was going to happen, and that it was time to let him go. Whether or not they saw themselves as handing over this trust to God, I do not know.

The legal processes which allowed food and water to be withdrawn, with the intention of letting him die, were prolonged and highly controversial. My own belief is that it would have been better to let him die of one of the infections which, if untreated, are sooner or later likely to kill such patients. Withdrawal of treatment is well recognised as an appropriate policy in hopeless cases. Withdrawal of food and drink, even if this has had to be given by artificial means, is a quicker but more morally dangerous alternative, in that it offends against the principle of ordinary minimal care. The distinction may seem a fine one, and many doctors are impatient with it, but similar fine distinctions are important in deciding where to draw the line against euthanasia. There are increasing and disturbing tendencies to help terminally ill patients on their way by not offering them food and drink, a policy which many believe offends in the most basic way against the relationship of trust between patients and the medical services.

On a Christian understanding, diminished personalities need special care. It is the duty of the strong to help the weak. The reason given for this may seem bizarre to those who do not share Christian convictions, and it offends against all good evolutionary principles, but it follows from what I have said about our all-encompassing relationship with God. In the case of the weak, there is less to obscure this relationship, and it is in caring for 'the little ones' that surprised believers learn that they have in fact been caring for Christ. St Paul has much to say about finding strength in weakness, because consciousness of weakness can allow a kind of transparency to God, which is much more difficult to discern in those who have more worldly reasons to feel full of themselves. St John's Gospel pushes the paradox to its limit in identifying the glory of God with Christ on the cross. It is this kind of thinking which underlies the much quoted comment that the quality of a society is to be judged by the way it treats its weakest members.

Before leaving the subject, I must return to Teilhard de Chardin with a tailpiece on the tendency towards cosmic pessimism, which nowadays seems to be replacing the 'onward and upward' philosophy described at the beginning of this chapter. We are solemnly told that life, civilisation and everything else must ultimately be futile, because one day an asteroid will hit us, or we shall pollute ourselves to death, or the sun will cool down, or the universe start contracting, or whatever. In other words, all that we know and value faces ultimate diminishment, albeit perhaps not for millions of years. Some regard this as the final proof that a good God could not have created a universe destined for destruction.

If there is any validity in what this chapter has said about the way God holds persons in being, despite earthly diminishment, then both the optimists and the pessimists are wrong. The universe is full of wonderful things which have permanent value for God because they have existed in time. The fact that time may be finite, just as space appears to be finite, does not lessen the value of either. Whether we are heading for Teilhard de Chardin's Omega point, or our world will one day be swallowed up in a black hole, is beside the point. What happens in the passage of time, in all its amazing complexity, retains its ultimate significance and worth, because the ever-present God cherishes each moment.

12

Knowing good and evil

In Kafka's parable from *The Trial*, recounted in Chapter 1, the man who waited all his life at the entrance to the law discovered only when he was dying that that particular gateway was intended exclusively for him. As the doorkeeper answered the man's final question about why no one else had come seeking admission, he closed the door. The priest who told the parable then went on to offer various contradictory interpretations, until K., the subject of the book, walked away in despair. It may seem far-fetched, but I was reminded of this story by some of the language used about one of the great scientific projects of the last decade of the twentieth century, the sequencing of the entire human genome. It has been described as the Holy Grail of biology, the key to the door of the ultimate knowledge of life.

The Human genome

The genome is the complete genetic structure of an organism, and sequencing is the unravelling of this structure down to the level of the individual amino acid bases which constitute, as it were, the letters of the so-called genetic code. Sequencing is more detailed than the mapping of genes which, to continue the analogy, may vary in size from a paragraph to a substantial book. Many of the genes themselves were long ago assigned to positions on the chromosomes, which on average are each roughly equivalent to half a complete set of the *Encyclopaedia Britannica*. Only a few genes have so far been completely sequenced. The entire genome, if written out with a letter for each base, would fill about ten sets of encyclopaedias, and contain some three billion letters. It would look mind-bogglingly dull, and could only be handled by powerful computers, but the elucidation of this law of our being, the search for the Holy Grail, is a goal so ambitious and magnetic that hundreds of scientists all over the world have been willing to devote years to what is in fact a boringly repetitive task.

So what will be its significance when it is complete? And might it, as in Kafka's parable, reveal its ambivalence as a goal of hitherto forbidden knowledge? The door stands open with all its promise and its threat. Like K., we may find ourselves condemned if we enter it, and condemned if we do not.

First, it is important to be clear what the code actually does. The genetic alphabet consists of only four letters, representing the four amino acid bases, hundreds of millions of which are strung out along immense strands of DNA, the self-replicating molecule found in the nucleus of almost every cell in the body. The bases function in groups of three, and can thus spell out a maximum of sixty-four ($4 \times 4 \times 4$) different, three-letter 'words'. Each word codes for one of twenty different amino acids which, depending on the order in which they are manufactured by the gene, combine to make the thousands of different proteins and enzymes which constitute all living organisms. The code is thus the first step in a body-building or body-maintaining process, which takes place as these proteins and enzymes react with, and relate to, one another. Their interactions are hugely complex, still for the most part only partially understood, and may be subject to many kinds of influence from their environment.

Some of the processes are very robust and minor alterations in the code have little effect on the end result. Others are highly sensitive, and a mistake as small as a single letter in a single gene can have lethal consequences, as happens for instance in cystic fibrosis. It is often pointed out that the genetic make-up of humans only differs by some two per cent from that of the higher apes, as if this indicates virtual identity between the species. In fact, in a system where the alteration of one letter in three billion might spell the difference between life and death, two per cent can represent a tremendous potential for difference. Also relevant is the curious fact that ninety-five per cent of the human genome is at present classified as junk, or at least as having no known biological function.

Paradoxically, the major genetic differences between individuals, and hence the most useful parts of the genome for the purposes of genetic identification, are located within this junk.

The motives for sequencing the junk in addition to those parts of the genome known to be significant are not entirely obvious, given the costs of the whole operation. But this brings us back to the Holy Grail concept, or as others have put it, the climbing Everest 'because it's there' syndrome. The lure of what lies at the end of the journey has proved irresistible.

Much of what is found will doubtless prove to be useful in the long run. The full sequence will provide a vast template against which genetic samples can be compared. This will make it easier to identify genes where something has gone wrong, and to develop techniques for remedying the defect. Knowing the sequence for a particular protein makes it possible to manufacture the protein by some alternative means, for example in genetically modified bacteria, a technique already used in the manufacture of insulin. Another technique involves replacing a defective section of a gene with a normal one, by the now familiar methods of cutting and splicing sections of DNA. It is in principle possible to go beyond the business of repairing identifiable defects, to making actual changes and hoped-for improvements in our genetic heritage; indeed this is already done with agricultural crops and animals, and is justified ethically as merely a sophisticated extension of breeding methods which are as old as humanity.

The fully sequenced genome will also provide a

powerful tool in the further study of evolution, as increasing numbers of species are subjected to detailed genetic comparison. It will enable human beings to take control of evolution in ways never contemplated before, and it has the potential to give every individual unique insight into their own genetic inheritance, and to order their lives in the light of that knowledge. As we shall see later, such foresight is already possible in assessing the susceptibility to cystic fibrosis. In short, reasonable, pragmatic aims can be cited in justification of the genome project, even though most of them could probably be accomplished with something less than the entire sequence. I suspect, however, that the vast efforts now being expended have, at their root, compulsions more akin to those of Kafka's character, in his readiness to spend his entire life in search of its ultimate secret, the secret of himself.

Will that be what he finds? The unmasking of the genome, as I have indicated, is only a first step towards understanding the complex processes of life itself. Even this first step has its elements of ambivalence. What might it mean in practice to know one's entire genetic constitution? If we concentrate for the present on disease-inducing defects in single genes, it is obvious that more extensive knowledge of the whole genome could bring great benefits to sufferers. There are some two thousand known defects of this kind, most of them very rare, but because each is linked to a single gene, they are in principle relatively easy to remedy. Sequencing is necessary to identify them, and complete sequencing might disclose more.

Genetic defects

The defect causing cystic fibrosis is among the most common and is carried by about one in twenty-five of the population. Since the defective gene in this case has to be carried by both parents before the disease can occur, the chances are that one in 625 (25×25) marriages will produce children at risk. Of these, by the ordinary rules of genetic inheritance, one is likely to be clear of the defect, two are likely to be carriers, and one is likely to suffer from the disease, thus making the overall incidence of the disease one in 2,500 (625×4) – which is what is actually found. Counter measures can, and have been, taken at each of the stages involved: counselling at the time of marriage, selective abortion after testing of the fetus, and gene therapy in children when the disease has manifested itself. At present the latter can only be done by conveying genetically modified DNA to the affected sites (mainly the lungs), a process which has to be repeated at regular intervals. A permanent cure could in principle be effected in the next generation, by repairing the defective gene in a fertilised ovum before it is implanted in the uterus. Such germ-line therapy, as it is called, has not yet been attempted, nor is it permitted, as it raises serious ethical problems to which we shall return later.

Another disease caused by a single genetic defect, Huntingdon's chorea, is more strongly inherited and even more devastating in its consequences. Unlike cystic fibrosis, it can be caused by a defective gene from only one parent, so the frequency of incidence in an affected family is higher. Moreover, since the disease does not appear until around the age of forty, parents have usually had their children before they know whether or not one of them carries the gene. Once the disease appears, swift degeneration and early death are the inevitable result. There is no cure, except the potential of germ-line therapy. Those who belong to families in which the disease is present face the agonising choice of whether to be tested, and perhaps live with the knowledge that they are doomed, or to refuse testing, and perhaps run the risk of transmitting the disease to another generation. I find it significant that one of the main researchers on Huntingdon's chorea, who works with a particularly vulnerable group of families in Venezuela and who herself belongs to a family in which the disease is present, decided not to be tested (at least not when I last heard about her work). It is a serious question whether there are some things it is better not to know.

Dangerous knowledge

One of the practical complications caused by knowledge of our genes is that it does not only affect those who acquire it. Our genes are the carriers of our physical relationship with one another. If I learn about some genetic defect in myself, I also learn that one of my parents almost certainly had it, and that one or more of my children will probably have it too. There may be other reasons, apart from the possibility of devastating diseases, for not welcoming such knowledge, and there have already been cases in which it has led to embarrassing questions about paternity, or agonising decisions about what to tell the children.

A further complication is that with the development of increasingly sophisticated DNA testing techniques, anybody can in theory be tested without their consent. A hair or a flake of skin is enough. I could, for instance, write to my insurance company refusing to be tested for some life-threatening hereditary condition, and if I had licked the envelope, they could do the test on that. I am not suggesting that this is what actually happens, except in criminal investigations. My general point is simply that knowledge is always ambivalent. The huge, and for the most part welcome, access of knowledge made possible by genetics may bring its own threats and disadvantages, and its own restrictions on freedom. We may suffer by acquiring it, and suffer if we do not.

Another danger is that we might presume that we know more than we do. I have so far referred to a limited number of conditions caused by changes in a single gene. The vast majority of our human capacities, individual quirks and deficiencies are not like that. They depend upon the interaction between numerous genes, and hence are much more difficult to track down and much less certain in their assignment to particular characteristics of particular genes, still less to identifiable variations in the genetic alphabet. In highly complex interactions of this kind there are uncertainties and degrees of freedom which do not exist in the one-to-one process of forming proteins from DNA templates.

It is wise, therefore, to be cautious about claims to have unearthed a gene for homosexuality, say, or heart disease, or alcoholism, or aggressiveness. It is possible that all these have a genetic component, just as fair hair, blue eyes, long noses and much else have usually been regarded as inherited. The family game of assigning a baby's qualities to its relatives is an unconscious acknowledgment of the extent to which our genes make us what we are. But the fact that it makes sense to assess odds in a completely deterministic fashion in the case of cystic fibrosis and Huntingdon's chorea is no argument in favour of genetic determinism in the much more complex circumstances where many genes are involved. It seems nearer the mark to say that they prescribe the states of being which are possible to us, but not necessarily what actually happens.

Studies on twins explored this highly controversial field long before anybody started the detailed analysis of genes. The comparison of identical twins separated at birth holds out the promise of being able to distinguish between the effects of heredity and those of the environment, the so-called balance between nature and nurture. In one such case two twins, Oskar and Jack, who had not only been separated at birth but had also been brought up on different sides of the world – one as a Christian in Germany, and the other as a Jew in Trinidad – showed astonishing similarities. Both arrived for investigation wearing double-breasted blue shirts with epaulettes; both had moustaches and wire-rimmed spectacles; both flushed the toilet before and after using it, kept rubber bands round their wrists, dipped buttered toast in their coffee, and enjoyed surprising people by sneezing in lifts. They had only met once before, two decades earlier.

The interest in this case lies in the extent to which their resemblances included quite trivial matters, which at first glance almost everyone would have assigned to their upbringing. The behavioural resemblances could be coincidence – but their case is by no means an isolated instance. It could be that some twins retain a form of non-material connection, perhaps via telepathy – but this is not a popular form of explanation among most scientists. It seems highly unlikely that there is a gene for wearing wire-rimmed spectacles, but it is possible to imagine how thousands of genes might work together to produce the kind of character which favours the simple look, or whatever it is that attracts people to wire rims.

Behaviour formation of such precision within such a complex genetic scenario would seem to imply a strong degree of genetic determinism, at least in some instances. But against this have to be set the large number of identical twins who, in much more important aspects of their character and temperament, turn out quite differently. Nor can these differences always be explained away in terms of nurture. Some early studies of newly born identical twins revealed temperamental differences even in the first few weeks of life. By contrast, a recent study of mental abilities in elderly twins claimed that, even after a lifetime of experience, heredity could still account for about sixty per cent of the characteristics being measured.

Clearly there is a great deal more to be discovered,

and as genetic research increases in volume there will be more and more newspaper headlines about the unearthing of the gene for this or that aspect of human behaviour. Hitherto most of such claims have not survived for long, partly for the reason already given: when one is dealing with an orchestra of genes rather than a single instrument, it is not easy to discern precisely which is doing what, or what the actual performance of the music adds to what was written in the score. Some claims have come unstuck because the researchers have picked on behavioural characteristics which may only have been identified fairly recently, and which may depend more on the scientific fashions of the moment than on some capacity or impulse built into our evolutionary inheritance. An earlier generation of geneticists looked for the hereditary components in 'pauperism, feeble-mindedness, nomadism, shiftlessness and eroticism'. Where are they now? Some of their successors have been busy sticking genetic tags on equally controversial and indefinable qualities such as 'intelligence'.

Genetic constraints

I argued in Chapter 9 that there is such a thing as human nature, and that its basic characteristics must have been formed in the course of evolution, but that in human beings most of our mental development takes places after birth. I start from the presupposition, therefore, that our genes must be important in shaping what we are, but far from exclusively so. Some aspects of behaviour may be inherited, others have to be learnt during the long process of nurturing required by humans. The cultural matrix in which certain types of behaviour are significant also has to be taken into account, alongside individual experience and the purely physical aspects of evolutionary change. There would not be much advantage, for instance, in developing a genetic basis for language in a culture where nobody spoke; nor would manual dexterity have been of much value unless our earliest ancestors had actually used tools. Nature and nurture, the givenness of our genes, the use we make of what we have been given, and the environment in which all this takes place, go hand in hand and are no more separable in detail than the ingredients of a cake.

There is another, more theological, reason for being sceptical about over-ambitious claims concerning genetic determinism, at least in human beings. I have argued throughout this book that one of our fundamental characteristics is our ability to stand outside what we are, to transcend ourselves. The acquisition of language seems to have unleashed this ability, but the very fact that this was possible as a development within the process of evolution seems also to tell us something about the kind of reality with which we are dealing. The likelihood, for instance, that the universe is not as deterministic as machine-based analogies once seemed to imply, leaves room for the belief that there is an open-endedness about the way things are, an inherent possibility of novelty and creativity, which can give extra credence to our own awareness of freedom. This same sense of openness and awareness of freedom finds expression, in Christian thought, in the possibilities of self-transcendence implicit in our relationship with God. It is as if at one end of the scale of existence reality is firmly rooted in sheer givenness, whereas at the other end the sky is the limit.

In summary, it seems reasonable to assume that our genes shape our propensities and set constraints on us. They provide our equipment for living, good, bad, or indifferent, as the case may be. But they do not, and cannot, determine what we make of the opportunities open to us.

Suppose this were not so. Suppose it were possible for each of us to obtain a complete read-out of our personal genome and, by feeding this into a computer, discover precisely what we might expect of life, what diseases will strike us and when, what skills we shall develop, how we shall react to this or that challenge, what we shall think and feel, and when we shall die. Is it the kind of knowledge any of us would want? Or would it in fact place an intolerable burden on us, reducing our life to a kind of puppetry? Kafka's man, at his own unique entrance to the law, wanted to penetrate the mysteries of what had been happening to him. Perhaps it was a mercy to him that he never did. At the heart of his problem lay the debilitating fear of being a mere puppet, trapped in a bureaucratic nightmare, a pawn in an inexorable process which intimately concerned him, yet in which he could be no more than a spectator.

The more balanced assertion that we have genetic propensities and greater or lesser degrees of freedom accords better with what we know of ourselves outside the spectre of Kafka's world. It may well be that some people are more constrained by their heredity than others. In general, though, freedom grows with the exercise of its correlate – responsibility. It is diminished every time responsibility is avoided, whether by blaming some failure on our enemies, circumstances, or genes. 'I can't help it!' may often, tragically, be true, but usually only as the end result of a long process of refusing to accept our actions as our own. To be aware of a propensity or predisposition, say to alcoholism, presents us not with a certainty, but with a choice. We can take it seriously and moderate our drinking, or cut it out altogether, or change our lifestyle, or our friends, or take any of a number of actions which might reduce the risk. Or we can ignore it. Worse still, we can accept the descent into alcoholism as inevitable, by the abdication of responsibility for it. Awareness of a propensity acts as a warning signal and a constraint, but it is the kind of constraint which may actually increase freedom by providing the context within which realistic choices are to be made. Such knowledge of ourselves is generally to be welcomed, provided we want it and are capable of responding to it. It is quite different from the knowledge that our fate is fixed.

It is worth noting also the strong element of self-contradiction in believing that our life is entirely determined by our genes, or by anything else in our constitution. It is the same argument we have met earlier in considering the nature of explanation. The logical implication of believing in genetic determinism would be that this belief, like every other, was determined simply by the way our genes happened to be. But from that it would follow that there was no good reason to suppose it was true. Arguments which deny human beings the freedom to think or behave rationally always collapse, because they undermine their own unexamined assumptions. Without the belief that it is possible to think freely and rationally, rational argument is not possible. In fact, most people know from direct experience that if they are told what somebody else has calculated they are bound to do, this acts as a powerful reason for not doing it. That is part of being human.

Do we then have absolute freedom, as this experience of confounding other people's certainties might suggest? The notion that choice could, and should, be totally unconstrained is equally unrealistic. It was made fashionable in the mid-twentieth century by existentialism, which dubbed freedom 'inauthentic' unless it was so unconstrained as to be arbitrary. Sartre, the high priest of the movement, followed Nietzsche in denying that there is anything essential to human nature; there are no constraints, he claimed, genetic or otherwise. He envisaged existential choice as being made in a kind of vacuum, as an act of self-creation. 'Man is nothing else but that which he makes of himself.'

The assertion of absolute freedom and the claim to self-creation are conceits which still linger on within a vociferous cultural fringe. They not only fly in the face of the biological facts, but ignore the experiential truth that genuine freedom must have its discipline, and that it is the constraints on us which are most likely to release our potential. An artist constrained to work with canvas and paint uses these as means through which to express what far transcends canvas and paint; but without the discipline inherent in their use, art can rapidly turn into self-indulgence. Poets testify to the value of metre and rhyme in forcing them into a creative disciplining of their thoughts. Isaiah Berlin, that great champion of freedom, has a fascinating essay in his last book, *The Sense of Reality*, on 'Kant as an unfamiliar source of nationalism'. His argument in a nutshell is that enlightened rationalism, as typified in Kant, stressed the primacy of free choice. Each of us lives by our values, because they are *ours*. But where do our values come from? We fool ourselves if we imagine that we have simply invented them. However much we may change them, their origin lies in the traditions and culture of the group in which we live, and the most pervasive conveyor of tradition and culture is the nation. The primacy of free choice, in other words, leads us back in the direction of nationalism – an unwelcome and surprising conclusion to those who affect to despise nationalism in the name of individuality.

Even in this highly compressed form, the argument invites a further question. If so-called free choice tends, albeit unconsciously, to find itself trapped in its own culture by the absence of values or constraints outside the self and its own particular environment, where are we to look for release? Are there liberating values and constraints embedded in some reality more fundamental than our own wills – in nature perhaps, in the givenness of things, even in God? Freedom without any acknowledged constraints quickly becomes bondage to unconscious forces and fashions, no less surely than constraints without freedom render life meaningless. To be aware of the constraints set by our genes, therefore, may actually increase, not diminish, the possibilities of realistic choice. It may also have other significances, not least in posing the question of whether it would ever be right deliberately to alter them.

Genetic manipulation

Except in the case of identical twins, genes, as the precursors of individual bodies, are the main physical basis of personal uniqueness. This is one reason for being extremely cautious about cloning human beings. It is fantasy to suppose that *completely* identical human beings could be created because, as we have seen, our individual life history contributes to a greater or lesser extent to what each of us becomes. But if twins often experience a strong psychological relationship with one another, presumably on the grounds of their genetic identity, this is likely to be equally true of clones. In their case, though, the relationship would be even more complex, given that the person cloned would not only be their twin, but also in a very literal sense their father and mother.

Cloning would also necessarily involve manipulation of the germ line of the individual concerned, even though the material for cloning may not actually be taken from the germ cells themselves. The technique used for Dolly the sheep entailed making DNA – which could in principle have been taken from any cell in the donor's body – behave as if it were in a germ cell. It therefore comes up against the general objections to germ-line therapy.

These are mostly practical, one of them being that manipulation of genetic material at the embryonic stage necessarily affects the life of a person not yet born, who is not therefore capable of giving consent. A second objection is that, in the present stage of knowledge genetic manipulation of a human embryo, particularly if it involved several genes, would constitute an unacceptable risk. The techniques would be unproven, the consequences of genetic change uncertain, and it is difficult to see how the risks could be reduced without performing experiments which would fall foul of the previous objection. Furthermore, the risks would not just be taken by the persons concerned, but would affect all their descendants. Thirdly, manipulation of the germ line, and cloning even more so, would also offend against the religiously based belief that our unique identity is somehow given to us and is not, as it were, to be exchanged for something else, or mass produced for some genetic supermarket. The safeguarding of our uniqueness can be seen as a corollary of the belief that we are known by God, and that our identity is held in being by him. The Chief Rabbi, Jonathan Sacks, has drawn attention to a quotation from the Mishnah which makes a similar point: 'When a human being strikes many coins from the same mould, they are all alike. The Holy One, blessed be He, creates human beings in His image, yet every one is different.'

Answers have been given to all these objections. Theologically it might be argued that human beings are in some measure co-creators with God. If it belongs to the essence of human nature that we strive to transcend ourselves, what can be the objection to seeking to manipulate and improve ourselves genetically? We do it all the time in other spheres of life, and have no compunction about doing it to our children. What moral difference is there between moulding a child's character by inducing it into certain behavioural patterns and moulding its genetic inheritance by deliberate interference? As for risks, these can be reduced by making haste slowly, by permitting only limited and carefully controlled experiments. If one of these was clearly going wrong, malformation could probably be spotted at an early stage and abortion, it is claimed, would provide the remedy. Nothing worthwhile is achieved without risk, and the medicine we have today would have been impossible unless doctors had been willing to experiment on the frontiers of knowledge. The birth of Louise Brown, the first IVF baby, entailed just such risks, and the scientists concerned had the courage to take them.

An objection which, in my view, cannot be so optimistically dismissed, draws on a deeper understanding of persons and how they relate to one another. The belief that persons are made for self-transcendence must not be interpreted as meaning that anyone else – even a prospective parent – has a right to play God with them. This is a potential which each person has to discover within themselves. To attempt the genetic improvement of one's offspring by manipulating them as embryos looks more like a form of self-gratification than a selfless desire to give them the best life possible. The element of self-gratification would be even more evident in any attempt to produce one's own clone.

Personal fulfilment depends on the mutual recognition of each person as Other. So does the possibility of becoming a moral being. Fundamental to a proper respect for persons, and hence to a moral relationship with them, is this acceptance of them in their givenness. It is not for nothing that we speak about babies as 'gifts', even though the process of fertilisation and bringing to birth may have involved much medical assistance. Would we feel the same, I wonder, if that assistance had included deliberate specification of the only kind of gift which would be acceptable? The issue is often discussed under the heading 'designer babies', but more is at stake than a criticism of the – surely limited – class of parents who think of babies as fashion accessories and will be content with nothing less than perfection. The central issue, as I have already indicated, is how we relate to other persons, even the youngest of them. Though we may frequently want to change other persons, and in the case of our own children to mould their characters by the way we treat them, this always involves relating to them as persons, not treating them as objects. By contrast, to manipulate an embryo is precisely to treat it as an object. It is to insert into our relationship with the person who grows from it an intervention which, however well meaning, touches the genetic core of that person's being and does not acknowledge its otherness.

A further consideration of abortion

This is difficult territory, bringing us back inevitably to the subject of abortion, which encapsulates all the key moral dilemmas concerning the roots of personhood. Does it make any sense to seek to identify a core of personality which must not be violated, and if so what are we looking for? Those who believe that abortion any time after the fusion of ova and sperm is the moral equivalent of murder must presumably be identifying this core with the just-formed set of chromosomes, since at this earliest stage the chromosomes comprise all that is new. According to this view, the new individual thus created achieves personal status, with all the appropriate rights and privileges, on the basis and from the moment of a simple genetic union, unless we are to imagine the infusion of a soul at this precise point in time – a concept whose difficulties I have already discussed. One might alternatively base an argument on God's intentions for this new set of chromosomes, and their potential to become a unique person.

On the other hand, the fact that a high proportion of fertilised ova are discarded by nature, and never become more than 'might-have-been' persons, must surely count against putting too much moral weight on the formation of a single, and probably ephemeral, new genetic combination out of the unimaginable number of those which are theoretically possible. The strict identification of new set of chromosomes with new person in fact seems to lead to absurdity. This was evident in the recent public outcry about the proposed destruction of frozen embryos created for the purposes of in-vitro fertilisation, which had passed the date by which they should have been used. There was much talk of 'lost babies', as if they were the victims of some pre-uterine holocaust. But it would be just as sensible to think of science mirroring nature in its wastefulness, the main difference lying in the fact that the natural wastefulness is usually not seen. Genes are cheap.

Human identity

This thought raises a further question, however. If genes are cheap, and if the core of personality is not to be identified with an individual genome, what grounds are there for treating the givenness of a new life with such respect, to the point of refusing to manipulate it genetically? The difference surely lies, not in what the new genome is at this earliest stage, but in what it is going to become. Every fertilised ovum faces a strong possibility that it will have no future. Its loss, therefore, even its destruction for a sufficiently serious reason, as in a conflict between two evils, may be regarded as morally acceptable. But if it were in some way manipulated, and allowed to develop into a person, that person would bear the marks of someone else's deliberate interference. Such interference, brought to fruition in an actual person, would inevitably affect their perception of themselves, as well as other people's perceptions of them; the sense of givenness would be threatened. The emotional difficulties experienced by transsexuals, and the ambivalent feelings of many people towards them, are a lesser example of what can happen when givenness is unclear or thrown in question.

The distinction I am drawing may seem over-subtle, but I believe it is fundamental. The point is that it is not the destruction or the manipulation of the genome itself which carries unacceptable moral consequences, but the significance of this manipulation for the person to whom the genome belongs and who will eventually develop from it. The first belongs within the realm of biochemistry; the second concerns a human life. This is the logic of allowing research to be done on very early embryos, provided that – and the proviso is crucial – they are never allowed to develop beyond this stage.

Genes are no more than strings of chemical instructions. Though they may carry the hopes of those who contributed them, and be in that sense highly valued, they are not in themselves valuable until many other developments have taken place. Furthermore, there are simply too many of them to make it a matter of great significance what happens to any particular set. A single human body contains trillions of sets of genes, one for almost every cell, nearly all of them carrying the complete instructions for a whole body. Germ cells are different only in that they use the instructions in a different way, and this is why they need to be treated more carefully and more respectfully, especially as they develop and begin to make their presence felt. The legal definition of the stage (at around 14 days) before which therapeutic research on them is permitted has some biological justification, in that this is roughly the time when those cells which are going to develop into the actual fetus differentiate themselves from the remainder. It is not until then that the body, as opposed to the genome, of the person-to-be can be said to have a firm identity. The definition is dismissed by some as a legal quibble invented to satisfy the needs of scientists, but that is a cynical dismissal of the attempt to make moral sense of some very complex biological processes, the fluidity of which at this earliest stage of development allows no clear meaning to terms like 'person' or 'core of personality'.

The strongest reason, however, for not giving overwhelming moral weight to the formation of a new set of genes at the moment when the male and female genes unite is that, although this marks the beginning of what may become a personal story, it is at that stage no more than a chemical reaction, albeit a wonderfully mysterious and potent one. Its moral significance begins to grow as other, personal qualities begin to emerge. Persistence in time, sensitivity, responsiveness, relatedness – all those subtle indications of otherness gradually make their presence felt and signal to the mother that the child in her womb is a being with an identity of its own. The core of personhood, one might say, is fashioned out of this responsiveness, which in Christian eyes finds its fulfilment in the possibility of responsiveness towards God. Soul-making and body-making go hand in hand. Thus it is that when we can recognise some of the marks of personhood, and be aware of an 'other' like ourselves, the sense of moral responsibility towards this 'other' becomes more and more pressing. Most people are not greatly exercised about the morality of morning-after pills, even though fertilisation may have taken place. But to destroy an 'other', with whom one has begun to relate in however minimal a sense, is a different matter altogether.

These issues also loom large on the genetic moral agenda because, in the present state of knowledge, the usual 'cure' following an early diagnosis of genetic defect is selective abortion. It is an option which has brought great hope and comfort to parents who are aware of their genetic risks, or have already had a child with a genetic defect and who dare not try again without some assurance that any child born to them will be normal. But abortion, especially when the fetus is large enough to be tested, carries a heavy moral and emotional price. If the hazards of germ-line therapy could be reduced to reasonable proportions, it might be argued that this would be a better option medically for the elimination of crippling hereditary diseases, and a better moral option too, despite the objections against interfering with genetic givenness. We do not hesitate to treat other bodily defects, so why should we draw the line at genes, provided the reasons are genuinely therapeutic?

A slippery slope?

There are some disturbing precedents, though. Once techniques have been perfected, they are likely to be used for all sorts of unintended purposes. As therapeutic surgery has paved the way for cosmetic surgery, may not germ-line therapy pave the way for germ-line cosmetics? How far is it right to go in the pursuit of normality, or beyond normality to perfection? If it proves possible to remedy the two thousand or so serious hereditary diseases linked with defects in single genes, what is to prevent more adventurous experiments, perhaps with multiple genes, perhaps with genes responsible for some major personal characteristics, with a view to 'improving' human nature? Any manipulation involving multiple genes would mean juggling with a frightening number of unknowns, but the fact that it might be possible strongly suggests that one day it will be attempted.

In a sense this is the story of mankind; the fruits of human ingenuity in manipulating what nature has provided for us have laid the foundations for civilised life. In our own day the genetic revolution has already had a huge impact on agriculture, and the commercial pressures to push out the boundaries of knowledge and to develop new products have set a cracking pace for change. In Britain nowadays it is difficult to avoid foods which at one stage or another have been genetically manipulated. Long-life tomatoes are one of the success stories, even though most people are unaware of what has been done to them in order to improve their shelf life.

From another perspective, it can be said that what is happening now, in the production of better crops and new breeds, is simply an acceleration of what has always been happening as farmers have experimented with cross-breeding and used, perhaps unconsciously, an implicit awareness of how heredity works. Back in Old Testament times we find Jacob doing it, in Genesis chapter 30, albeit by somewhat unorthodox means. As human beings we have done the same to ourselves, in the careful choice of husbands and wives. Substitute the word 'gene' for 'blood', and not much has altered over the centuries, except the rate and scale of change. The new techniques have enabled massive and pre-dictable genetic reorderings to be made, to a degree which is impossible under an ordinary programme of controlled breeding. The rate and scale of possible change are thus the really decisive factors which face our age with new opportunities and dilemmas. Previous experiments, including the grand experiment of evolution itself, have operated for the most part locally and over immensely long periods. Mistakes have had time to be ironed out, balancing factors have had time to develop, and disasters have only on rare occasions been global. Today's experiments are much less haphazard, but they carry greater risks. The world is smaller, time for the assimilation of change is shorter, and the leaps into unknown territory are more adventurous. That is why genetic issues are likely to be high on the world's moral agenda for a long time to come, and why public anxieties about what is happening need to be taken seriously. In particular, it seems to me, some means has to be found to restrain the strong commercial pressures which tend to drive technological developments faster than the well-proven science and the public moral awareness which should undergird them.

In this chapter I have done no more than indicate some of the complex questions raised by this new knowledge of ourselves. There is much that is exciting in it, and much that needs careful control. In the Genesis story, the tree of the knowledge of good and evil turns out to be as ambivalent as Kafka's entrance gate to the law. Eating from it represented an act of defiance and a loss of innocence – the source of 'all our woe', as Milton described it. Yet it was also a step into adulthood, into taking responsibility and suffering the consequences of it. The poet Edwin Muir, who wrote of both Milton and Kafka, described himself as having still 'one foot in Eden'; yet 'the other land' bears 'flowers in Eden never known'.

> What had Eden ever to say
> Of hope and faith and pity and love
> Until was buried all its day
> And memory found its treasure trove?
> Strange blessings never in Paradise
> Fall from these beclouded skies.
>
> ('One Foot in Eden', 1956)

We have met the same paradox with Elizabeth Jennings, in her nostalgia for Eden and her awareness that there is, nonetheless, no return to it through neatness, through meticulous control, because that would be to 'care in the wrong way'. Our modern capacities to tend, and to ruin, what God has given us are awesome. All the more important, then, to know what persons are and where our limitations should lie.

Why persons matter

The waiters set a leg of mutton before Alice, who looked at it rather anxiously, as she had never had to carve a joint before.

'You look a little shy; let me introduce you to that leg of mutton,' said the Red Queen. 'Alice – Mutton: Mutton – Alice.' The leg of mutton got up in the dish and made a little bow to Alice; and Alice returned the bow, not knowing whether to be frightened or amused.

'May I give you a slice?' she said, taking up the knife and fork, and looking from one Queen to the other.

'Certainly not,' the Red Queen said very decidedly: 'it isn't etiquette to cut anyone you have been introduced to. Remove the joint!'

We have already met Alice's leg of mutton as an illustration of the absurdities of Victorian etiquette. As so often in Lewis Carroll's fantasies, however, the questioning of ordinary assumptions and conventions can pave the way for deeper insights into the strange qualities of human life. To cut someone who has just been introduced to us (in both senses of the word 'cut') is to deny the significance of the relationship just formed. An introduction is an act of recognition of the other, and as such it carries moral obligations. These may be of a minimal kind as when, after an unwelcome introduction to some guest at a party, we seek to move on as soon as possible. Or the obligations may be enormous, as when a flicker of recognition of another's humanity, say by a guard in a concentration camp, imposes a weight of moral responsibility which may be soul destroying. To acknowledge somebody as a person carries with it the implication that they matter. Being a person and mattering are two sides of the same coin.

It is a conjunction of ideas which crops up all over the place. There is a nice illustration in Antoine de Saint-Exupéry's classic story, *The Little Prince*. The little prince meets a fox which asks to be tamed. 'One only understands the things one tames,' says the fox. 'Men have no more time to understand anything. They buy things all ready made at the shops. But there is no shop anywhere where one can buy friendship, so men have no friends any more. If you want a friend, tame me . . .' And that is just what happens. 'He was only a fox like a hundred thousand other foxes,' remarks the little prince, 'but I have made him my friend, and now he is unique in all the world.' Taming carries obligations, too, as the little prince discovers. 'Men have forgotten this truth,' says the fox later in the story, 'but you must not forget it. You become responsible, forever, for what you have tamed.'

In the early 1960s, in my first book, I had the temerity to write a chapter on computers and artificial intelligence. It was a time when optimism about being able to match human intelligence was riding higher than it is today. Thirty-five years later the difficulties concerning logic, referred to in Chapter 8, appear more daunting and the way forward less obvious. Successful chess-playing computers were not then on the cards, but even today's super-intelligent chess playing in no way matches the breadth and flexibility of human intelligence, because the computer is programmed for only one highly circumscribed and logically specifiable function. Back in the '60s, however, I made the point that if a process, even one as complicated as thinking, could be broken down into parts which were thoroughly understood, then in principle there should be no difficulty about reproducing it. In such a process of reproduction it should make no difference whether the functions were being performed in a brain or in a computer.

Given this possibility, as it then seemed, of building a computer with the equivalent of human intelligence, real questions would arise about how it should be treated, whether it would have to be regarded as being conscious, and what our moral responsibility towards it would be. My answer was that this would depend on whether we were willing to admit it as a member of the human club. There is no independent means of deciding what its moral status would be. Mere calculating power, however remarkable, would not confer such a status, if in the end our attitude towards it could still be summed up in the words, 'It's only a machine,' and if in principle we were still willing to pull out the plug. But if we were to acknowledge a degree of humanness, a character and quality of thinking like that of an independent mind, then we might also have to acknowledge a moral claim. It is the same principle at work as in the taming of animals, whereby we invest some of our humanness in the life of another creature. It is the step Frankenstein refused to take, thus condemning his creature to implacable opposition.

At the other end of the human scale, there is a good example of the inseparability of acknowledging and valuing in the *Warnock Report on In-Vitro Fertilization*. When faced with the question of what an embryo is, the committee wrote,

> Although the questions of when life or personhood begin appear to be questions of fact susceptible of straightforward answers, we hold that the answers to such questions in fact are complex amalgams of factual and moral judgements. Instead of trying to answer these questions directly we have therefore gone straight to the question of *how it is right to treat the human embryo.*

It was a decision which aroused much criticism during the subsequent debates, but it is difficult to see how else the committee could have proceeded. Its refusal to separate out the amalgam was vindicated by the fact that in the parliamentary debates speaker after speaker attempted to defend what purported to be factual judgments on what were actually moral grounds.

It would be possible to go on multiplying examples, but I hope the point is sufficiently made that questions of worth and questions about how we understand ourselves as persons are intimately related. It is a particular case of the more general realisation that fact and value are not always as rigidly distinct from one another as some philosophers once believed them to be, and as many scientists still assume they are.

Throughout this book I have been illustrating the development of self-understanding within the Western tradition, and how in different periods of history this has been shaped by the ideas and experiences of some of the tradition's most influential thinkers. The picture which has emerged is a complex and shifting one, with different emphases coming to the fore at different times and having different practical consequences. The various meanings given to the word 'person' capture these changes, and as I have discussed these I have spelt out a few of the consequences by constantly reverting to the same acute moral dilemmas at the beginning and end of life. Abortion and PVS pose questions about what a person is, and what worth such a person is perceived as having, at the extreme edges of human existence.

In describing somebody as a person, it might seem as if they are being measured against a list of possible attributes. Certainly there could be such a list, and it would contain such qualities and capacities as bodily distinctness, individuality, rationality, intentionality, autonomy, responsiveness, relatedness, consciousness, natural instincts, irreducibility, and less fathomable capacities such as openness towards God and the possibilities of self-transcendence. A person might be deficient in any or most of these – even bodily distinctness, as in the case of Siamese twins – but deficiencies need not imply lack of personhood, provided at least some criteria are met. In considering the moral status of embryos I suggested that the minimum criterion of individual existence should be the differentiation of those cells which are actually going to become the embryo. Even that is controversial, though, and there are others who would specify the chemical reaction whereby the new human genome is formed. In the case of Tony Bland there came a point at which the residual signs of personhood were not strong enough for his parents to go on wanting him to survive in a state of complete unresponsiveness. Their emotional ties could no longer sustain a one-sided relationship. They wanted to clarify it, by relating to him as being dead. At the end of three long years, there seemed to be nothing left except a body in a hospital. But that was controversial too, especially when it came to deciding what to do with a still living body whose interests could no longer be determined, because there seemed to be no person whose interests they were.

So how are we to judge? If perceptions of personhood have changed through the ages, and if lists of criteria can always be pared down or disputed, does the identification of someone as a person who matters by virtue of their personhood offer any real guidance?

Suppose we start instead with an extreme example of 'mattering' – being in love. To love someone is not to tick off a list of attributes, decide that they meet the right criteria, and then agree with oneself that this paragon among creatures is worth pursuing. Things might start like that, of course. A blind date might be no more than a time for mutual assessment. 'I don't like her nails'; 'His accent is awful'; 'I wish she was blonde', and so forth. But the sense of supreme worth, which is one of the symptoms of genuine love, goes far beyond any such assessment and in the end is speechless. This is why lovers grasp helplessly at poetry. 'Why do I love him/her?' 'Because he/she is who he/she is.' It is as simple and as complex as that. Translating it into the language I have used elsewhere, we might talk about encountering, acknowledging and loving the 'other' – the whole person as known and responded to in their 'otherness'. Being aware of the other was the key to Kant's theory of ethics; it is the acknowledgment of other people as 'ends in themselves', and hence as having moral worth.

Kant, in fact, provides one of the key philosophical links between being a person and mattering. He based it on rationality, in typical Enlightenment fashion. His foundation principle was that morality should be universal – what applies to ourselves should apply equally to everyone else. Since 'rational nature exists as an end in itself', rational beings should thus always be treated as ends in themselves and never simply as a means to an end. A universal morality demands that as we value our own ends, so we should respect other people as themselves having ends of their own. Perhaps we might gloss this rather austere formulation by describing persons as each having his or her own moral vantage point. They are centres of significance to themselves, and as such are unique and necessarily different. This is their 'otherness', and the Kantian argument can persuade us that they are 'others' who matter.

The notion of the 'other' needs, of course, to be fleshed out, and this is why the history of the concept of personhood is important, and why the practical implications of 'mattering' must depend, at least to some extent, on what persons are believed to be. But the bare sense of obligation, the recognition that here is a being to be respected, does not rest on a description of what persons are, but on something more elusive and fundamental – the demonstration of a presence. Wittgenstein wrestled with this problem in drawing his famous distinction between what can be *said* and what can only be *shown*. Philosophy, as he saw it, reveals the limits of language, but there are experiences beyond language which, he said, 'seem to those who have had them, for instance to me, to have in some sense an intrinsic, absolute value'. In a similar manner other persons can face us with a sense of absolute, intrinsic value. At least, they can unless inadequate concepts of personhood have conditioned us not to recognise it. I suggest, therefore, that it is not just for fleshing out the concept of the 'other' that an adequate understanding of the attributes of personhood can be seen to be necessary. It is, much more crucially, necessary if the capacity to acknowledge and respond to personal 'otherness' is to be kept open, and the raw awareness in face of the other thereby protected.

There is a parallel here with the protective function of theological language about God, much of which is negative – God is not finite, not corporeal, not limited by space and time. As in our acknowledgment of persons, it is the false and limiting concepts which have to be stripped away if we are to begin to grasp the true otherness of God. Language about persons cannot be taken to these extremes, but the history of the word is a warning against over-simplification. Persons are not just individuals, not just clever animals, not just social constructs, not just minds or bodies, consciousness or electrical impulses. They inhabit all these categories and transcend them as 'others' who matter.

This still leaves a problem. What is this bare presence of the other, which has to be demonstrated, 'shown' in the Wittgenstinian sense, rather than described or argued about? What is the minimum necessary in order to recognise that the one with whom we have to do is another human being? It seems to me that on this level, being conceived and born of human parents is the bottom line. It is the essential condition for recognising kinship, 'one of us', what I described earlier as 'being a member of the club'. It is the most immediate and obvious differentiation between us and all other animals and all human artefacts.

If that sounds like the attitude which some people condemn as 'speciesism' – giving moral priority to human beings over all other species – so be it. It need not entail devaluing other animals, or failing to acknowledge that they have legitimate interests of their own which ought to be respected. We can recognise, too, that animals may be even more mysteriously 'other' than our fellow human beings. But their otherness belongs to a different order, a pattern of relatedness of which we are not a part. There cannot be a mutuality of obligations between ourselves and other animals, however much we may feel responsible for them and want to protect them. Except in the case of those we have tamed, their otherness, in fact, is a totally alien otherness, not that mixture of empathy and difference which makes our encounter with other human beings so distinctive.

If we accept being born of human parents as representing the bottom line of morally significant personhood, this has further implications for what might or might not be acceptable concerning the processes of human generation. I have already said enough about the issues which arise before birth, the need to acknowledge increasing degrees of personhood in the growing fetus, and the moral obligations entailed by this. In fact, awareness of the presence of a significant other, with whom it is possible to form a prenatal relationship, brings forward the raw sense of obligation to an earlier stage in pregnancy when difficult questions of a more qualitative kind might have to be asked. Is the growing fetus deformed? And if it is, what degree of deficiency in the fleshed-out qualities of personhood is sufficient to outweigh the raw obligation to an other in process of formation? This is one of those instances when the current perception of personhood in a particular culture sets the conditions for acknowledging fundamental obligations. It is the truth behind the statement that the moral quality of a society is judged by its attitude towards abortion.

As we saw in the previous chapter, abortion is not the only issue in which that essential recognition of the other at the heart of our valuing might be obscured. How much prenatal genetic manipulation might be acceptable, for example, before whatever has been conceived ceases to be thought of as a mysterious other and becomes a manufactured article? It is a question which cannot be answered in our present state of knowledge, but it is not for nothing that Aldous Huxley located the beginnings of his *Brave New World* in a human hatchery. The most effective forms of depersonalisation start early.

A striking example of the bottom line of morally significant personhood at the other end of life is the Tomb of the Unknown Soldier in Westminster Abbey. It is a memorial to one whose every known attribute of personhood has been deliberately stripped away, so that he can represent soldierhood as a whole. What matters, and what the tomb celebrates, is that here is a soldier of whom nothing is known except that he died in war.

I return, finally, to what I have called 'fleshing out', the two millennia of reflection on the nature of personhood which have both enriched and at times distorted the basic perception that persons matter. We are what Charles Taylor has called 'self-interpreting animals', whose characteristic is to reflect on what we are, and who shape our aspirations in terms of our understanding – which is never complete. The story of how we have reached our present self-understanding should ideally form an essential part of that reflection, if only as a reminder that it is a continuing process, in which different forms of understanding have to be held in tension. We are cast by circumstances and by birth into roles and relationships on which we depend for our identity, but from which we also have to escape in order to be ourselves.

We are individuals, increasingly in these days conscious of our autonomy and freedom. We are also reminded that we could not be persons at all apart from the relationships with others which have shaped us and within which we have to go on discovering who and what we are. We have to be loved into personhood, and find our greatest fulfilment in loving others. We are not programmed as human animals, but neither can we afford to ignore our evolutionary inheritance. We have the possibility of transcending ourselves, but we are also bound by the laws of our being. We are often enigmas to ourselves and to each other, divided creatures with huge aspirations and capable of extraordinary wickedness. We reach for the stars, but find it hard to express what lies closest to our hearts. We can do wonderful and terrible things, and survive the loss of most of what seems to make life worth living.

Only religious imagery can do justice to the paradoxical heights and depths of being a person. Our identity, our continuity, our value, all that matters about us, are ultimately what they are as they are held in the mind of God. This is why the most obvious and familiar description remains the best. We are made in the image of God, and that contains both an assertion and a promise. 'Beloved, we are God's children now; it does not yet appear what we shall be, but we know that when he appears we shall be like him, for we shall see him as he is' (1 John 3:2).

For further reading

This is in no sense a complete bibliography. My hope is that it will be useful to those who want to explore topics further, or to know some of the books which have shaped my own thinking. Apart from the first three general classics, I have grouped the books according to chapters. Some of them refer to matters discussed in more than one chapter.

Classics

The Confessions of St Augustine. Book X is the most relevant.

René Descartes, *A Discourse on Method*, and the first two *Meditations*.

Blaise Pascal, *Pensées*. It is best to dip into Pascal, rather than to try to read him straight through. Avoid his lengthy biblical expositions!

Chapter 1

Bruno Bettelheim, *The Informed Heart: The human condition in modern mass society*, Thames and Hudson, 1960. Particularly interesting in view of the author's experience in one of the early Nazi concentration camps.

Morton N. Cohen, *Lewis Carroll*, Macmillan, 1995. Good on Carroll as a logician.

Erich Heller, *The Disinherited Mind*, Harmondsworth, 1961. An introduction to Kafka and Nietzsche. Kafka's *The Trial* is, of course, a must.

Chapter 2

Personal Origins, Second edition, 1996, a Church of England Board for Social Responsibility Report. An excellent, simple introduction to the whole subject of 'persons'.

Andrew Grubb *et al.*, *Doctors' views on the management of patients in persistent vegetative state*, 1997. A King's College London study of a subject on which not much has been written outside specialist works. A general review of the Bland case can be found in the report of the *House of Lords Select Committee on Medical Ethics*, 1994.

Norman M. Ford, *When did I begin?*, CUP, 1988. A detailed study of embryonic formation from a Roman Catholic perspective.

Chapter 3

The first two titles listed set the scene for the whole of this book.

Arthur Peacocke and Grant Gillett (eds.) *Persons and Personality*, Blackwell, 1987. Essays on philosophy, science, theology etc.

Charles Taylor, *Sources of the Self: The making of the modern identity*, CUP, 1989. A major historical and philosophical study, which has provided the framework for much subsequent writing about our self-understanding as persons.

Colin Gunton, *The One, the Three and the Many: God, Creation and the Culture of Modernity*, CUP, 1993. Usefully sets the doctrine of the Trinity in the sort of historical framework laid out by Taylor.

Austin Farrer, *The Glass of Vision*, Dacre, 1948. A study in the development of biblical symbolism.

C.C.J. Webb, *God and Personality*, Allen and Unwin, 1918. A classic, especially useful for its lucid account of the early development of the word 'person'.

John D. Zizioulas, *Being as Communion*, St Vladimir's Seminary Press 1985. Chapter 1 is a much quoted exposition of trinitarian doctrine in Eastern Orthodoxy.

Chapter 4

Karl Barth, *Church Dogmatics III 2*, 45, pp. 231–42, T. & T. Clark, 1960. An argument with Nietzsche about the nature of humanity.

Henry Chadwick, *Boethius: The Consolation of Music, Logic, Theology and Philosophy*, OUP, 1981.

Vladimir Lossky, *The Mystical Theology of the Eastern Church*. James Clarke, 1957. An Orthodox exposition.

Chapter 5

John Macmurray, *Persons in Relation*, Faber and Faber, 1961. Also referred to in the next chapter.

Michael Polanyi, *Personal Knowledge: Towards a post-critical philosophy*, Routledge and Kegan Paul, 1958. A major work in the philosophy of science, particularly well known for its description of 'tacit knowledge'.

Chapter 6

Steven Connor, *Postmodernist Culture: Introduction to theories of the contemporary*, Blackwell, 1989. A wide-ranging review with emphasis on the Arts and popular culture.

Friedrich Nietzsche, *The Genealogy of Morals*, 1887. Nietzsche is too large a subject to be represented by a single book, but this probably provides the best introduction to his style and characteristic themes.

Larry Rasmussen, *Moral Fragments and Moral Community*, Fortress Press, 1993. Contains a vivid description of the changing concepts of community in American society.

David Riesman *et al.*, *The Lonely Crowd: A study of the changing American character*, Doubleday, 1950.

Sherry Turkle, *Life on the Screen: Identity in the age of the Internet*, Weidenfield and Nicolson, 1996.

Chapter 7

John Bowker, *Is God a Virus? Genes, Culture and Religion*, SPCK, 1995. Also relevant to Chapters 9 and 12. Contains an interesting analysis of sociobiology, and a critique of Richard Dawkins.

Christopher Wills, *The Runaway Brain: The Evolution of Human Uniqueness*, HarperCollins, 1994. An accessible and informative – and slightly idiosyncratic – account of human evolution.

Daniel C. Dennett, *Consciousness Explained*, Allen Lane, 1992.

Daniel C. Dennett, *Darwin's Dangerous Idea: Evolution and the meanings of life*, Allen Lane, 1995. Dennett is a robust materialist philosopher, much criticised by his peers, but a great purveyor of ideas. His books are unfortunately very long, but full of sparkle.

Rom Harré, *The Singular Self: An introduction to the psychology of personhood*, Sage, 1998. An interesting essay in 'discursive psychology', making the point that persons are constituted by the conversations, internal and external, in which they take part. It is an idea, owing much to Wittgenstein, which is capable of theological extension.

Steven Mithen, *The Prehistory of the Mind: A search for the origins of art, religion and science*, Thames and Hudson, 1996.

Iris Murdoch, *The Sovereignty of Good*, Routledge and Kegan Paul, 1970. Some interesting ideas on the relation between attention and freedom.

Chapter 8

Keith Devlin, *Goodbye, Descartes: The end of logic and the search for a new cosmology of the mind*, Wiley, 1997. Contains an admirably clear account of the history of logic from Aristotle to Artificial Intelligence.

Mary Midgley, *The Ethical Primate: Humans, freedom*

and morality, Routledge, 1994. A typically robust critique of scientific reductionism, leading up to an evolutionary account of the development of human freedom. An excellent read.

Steven Pinker, *The Language Instinct: The new science of language and mind*, Penguin, 1994. A very readable exposition of Chomsky's theories about language. Controversial, but important.

Charles Taylor, *Human Agency and Language*, CUP, 1985. Philosophical papers, including useful chapters on 'The Concept of a Person' and 'Language and Human Nature'.

Ludwig Wittgenstein. For those who do not know him, the best approach is probably through Ray Monk's biography, *Wittgenstein*, Vintage, 1990. The book mentioned in this chapter is *Tractatus Logico-Philosophicus*, 1922, of which it was written,

> Said Wittgenstein: 'Don't be misled!
> What *can* be shown, cannot be said.'
> He aimed to be sensible,
> Not incomprehensible,
> But wrote the *Tractatus* instead.

Chapter 9

John Hick, *Evil and the God of Love*, Macmillan, 1966. An exposition of the 'Irenaean' approach to sin.

Philip Kitcher, *Abusing Science: The case against creationism*, MIT Press, 1982. A must for those tempted to think of creationism as scientific.

Andrew Linzey and Tom Regan, *Animals and Christianity: A book of readings*, SPCK, 1989. A useful anthology – both ancient and modern.

Mary Midgley, *Beast and Man: The roots of human nature*, Revised edition, Routledge, 1995. A superb book, relevant to much of this one, and with many wise things to say about sociobiology.

James Miller, *The Passion of Michel Foucault*, HarperCollins, 1993. An intellectual biography which sets Foucault's ideas about 'transgression' in the context of his life.

Keith Thomas, *Man and the Natural World: Changing attitudes in England 1500–1800*, Allan Lane, 1983.

E.O. Wilson, *On Human Nature*, Harvard, 1978. A much criticised attempt to apply the insights of sociobiology to human behaviour. His auto-biography, *Naturalist*, (Island Press, 1994), is an interesting example of how an early reaction against fundamentalist religion made him incapable of taking any religious claims seriously – a not un-common phenomenon. The same could be said of Richard Dawkins.

Chapter 10

Paul Davies, *The Mind of God: Science and the search for ultimate meaning*, Simon and Shuster, 1992. A response to Stephen Hawking. Do the laws of nature 'exist' in the mind of God?

David Hay, *Exploring Inner Space: Is God still possible in the twentieth century?* Revised Edition, Mowbray, 1987. A scientific analysis of religious experience. A later book, *Religious Experience Today*, (Mowbray, 1990), summarises the work of the Alister Hardy Research Centre.

David Jenkins, *The Glory of Man*, SCM, 1967. 'Jesus Christ is the reality of man who confronts us with the reality of God.'

Arthur Peacocke, *Theology for a Scientific Age: Being and becoming – natural, divine and human*, SCM, 1993. A systematic attempt to rethink Christian theology in the light of science. Top-down causation features prominently.

Keith Ward, *God, Chance and Necessity*, Oneworld, 1996. A vigorous and very readable attack on scientific materialism.

G.F. Woods, *Theological Explanation*, Nisbet, 1958. A much neglected book, written when linguistic philosophy was in fashion, and making the point that ultimate categories of explanation are personal.

Chapter 11

Paul S. Fiddes, *The Creative Suffering of God*, Clarendon, 1988. A demanding piece of theology for those who want to engage seriously with a Christian understanding of suffering.

Helen Oppenheimer, *The Hope of Happiness: A sketch for a Christian humanism*, SCM, 1983 and *Looking Before and After*, Collins, 1988. Both books explore sensitively what it is in us that can rise above disaster, and why people matter.

Pierre Teilhard de Chardin, *The Phenomenon of Man*, Collins, 1959 and *Le Milieu Divin: An essay on the interior life*, Collins, 1960. After the initial controversies there has been a more positive appreciation of Teilhard's work from the point of view of a biologist in Edward O. Dodson's *The Phenomenon of*

Man Revisited, Columbia University Press, 1984.

Chapter 12

Michael Mulkay, *The Embryo Research Debate: Science and the politics of reproduction*, CUP, 1997. A sociological analysis of the parliamentary debates.

Michael J. Reiss and Roger Straughan, *Improving Nature? The science and ethics of genetic engineering*, CUP, 1996. An excellent popular introduction to the genetic revolution by a biologist and a moral philosopher.

Tom Wilkie, *Perilous Knowledge: The Human Genome Project and its implications*, Faber and Faber, 1993. A good read, by a science journalist.

Chapter 13

John Puddefoot, *God and the Mind Machine: Computers, artificial intelligence and the human soul*, SPCK, 1996. Good on computers, but not so good on minds.

Abraham J. Heschel, *Who is Man?*, OUP, 1966. A Jewish scholar's meditation. 'Who is man? A being in travail with God's dreams and designs, with God's dream of a world redeemed, of reconciliation of heaven and earth, of a mankind which is truly His image, reflecting His wisdom, justice and compassion. God's dream is not to be alone, to have mankind as a partner in the drama of continuous creation. By whatever we do, by every act we carry out, we either advance or obstruct the drama of redemption; we either reduce or enhance the power of evil.'